PRAISE FC
KIM HERMANSON

Kim's work is absolutely path-breaking. She guides us to access source energy within our body and our being. Through image, sensation, and metaphor, we experience a place of deep knowing and non-polarity. This embodied experience of source energy/deep wisdom creates the shifts needed in both my inner and outer worlds with ease. In our work together I've gained immense clarity on my unique path and my unique gift. For the first time in my life, I feel a sense of alignment and flow, not as one-off moments of grace, but rather as my preferred way of being. Lately in our work together, I've been so excited to witness this energy at work not just in my personal process but in the larger collective as well. I can see how invaluable Kim's work is, in this moment, given the devastation we are witnessing in our world.

~ BRINDA JACOB-JANVRIN, FOUNDER,
STUDIO FOR MOVEMENT ARTS &
THERAPIES TRUST

When I work with Kim, I get a depth of understanding that goes far beyond my mind or even my heart. Images arrive spontaneously and they speak to me through a very strong felt sense that causes a powerful and transformative shift of my whole being. Her sessions are a deeply profound spiritual experience. Quite literally, they are life-changing.

~ MIM KOHN, DEPT. OF TEACHING & LEARNING, NEW YORK UNIVERSITY

I've been deeply involved in the Jungian movement for more than fifty years, and during those fifty years, I have worked with many world-renowned teachers. In the very first session with Kim, I immediately saw an inner image. It's the first time in all these years that I was able to do that. She's the real deal.

~ J.G.

I've done a lot of dream-work, active imagination, and imagery work, and nothing goes as deep. What Kim does shifts me at my core. When she speaks, I have an immediate change of energy. The energies and truth of her words flood in immediately and I enter into a different state of mind. Her work has created changes in my inner and outer worlds that I wasn't even aware that I needed. It's profound.

~ BRIGID BARRETT, RN, CONSULTANT AT BARRETT HOLISTIC SERVICES

DEEP
KNOWING

ENTERING THE REALM
OF NON-ORDINARY
INTELLIGENCE

DEEP KNOWING

KIM HERMANSON

Deep Knowing: Entering the Realm of Non-Ordinary Intelligence

ISBN-13: 978-1-7377920-0-0

Cover and Interior Design: *the*BookDesigners
Author Photograph: Susan Adler
Production: *the*BookDesigners

PUBLISHER:
Rawberry Books
1260 Hopkins Street
Berkeley, CA 94702

For my mother, whose life was about beauty.

CONTENTS

PREFACE

Since the Enlightenment, our view of
what is real has been organized around
the hegemony of a technological and materialistic
worldview... [our] mind-set has made the
very idea of other worlds unthinkable.

~ SUZI GABLIK, *The Enchantment of Art*

Over the course of my life, I've experienced non-ordinary realms, alternative states of consciousness, and a variety of encounters with Divine energies. Although I didn't know it at the time, I now understand three of these experiences to be shamanic initiations. In general, although I often enjoyed the startling potency of my encounters with the Spirit realm, I dismissed them. There was no place inside me to "put" these unusual occurrences. I had no spiritual mentor, no guru, no shamanic teacher, framework, or theory where any of it made sense.

Each of the three shamanic initiations involved a difficult test that brought me to the brink of physical or spiritual death. And in each case, I was able to survive the ordeal by entering an intelligent vibrational field and drawing upon its power.

I was a tough subject. It wasn't until Spirit gripped me with a third and final shamanic initiation—an encounter that rattled me to my core—that I came to a point where I could no longer dismiss my own experiences.

Something was being requested of me.

I spent the following years on an inner journey, developing the work contained in these pages. I hope that I've answered the call and that I've done it justice.

The shamanic initiations confirmed without a shadow of a doubt that there exists an intelligent field of energy that sincerely wants to help us. This realm is wise, powerful, and otherworldly; its healing gifts are not ordinary. It's also exquisitely beautiful.

Still, I felt that whatever Spirit was asking of me, I was the wrong person.

I'm the last person to teach about how we humans can enter mystical realms. I grew up in a conservative Midwestern family—a world away from anything remotely "new age." My friends and family never spoke of non-ordinary reality and I certainly wasn't going to attract their scrutiny. My conventional upbringing was solidly grounded in Midwestern practicality, hard work, and the value of science and rational thought. I graduated from a large state university with a degree in computer science and went to work in a corporation. That was the family trajectory. I wasn't about to question it.

However, for as long as I can remember, I've wanted to understand how adults learn. Upon entering the computer science field, my interest quickly shifted to artificial intelligence. I researched how experts know so that I could program that process into a computer. The first shamanic initiation occurred during this time. I share more about it in Chapter 1, but for now I will say that the experience sparked drastic change.

It was as if I had suddenly been plucked from one life and plopped down into a completely different one.

In this new life, I had the incredible opportunity and financial means to attend the University of Chicago to get a Ph.D. in adult learning. This opportunity was beyond anything I ever would have dreamed could happen for me.

At the university, I received a second surprising and extraordinary gift: the opportunity to be mentored by Mihaly Csikszentmihalyi, the author of the *New York Times* bestseller *Flow: The Psychology of Optimal Experience* and many other books. His pioneering work on flow largely initiated the positive psychology field and launched alternative research methods within the academic community.

Mihaly taught in the Psychology department and had no reason to be interested in me. He and his work were world-renowned. He was very busy and surrounded by lots of enthusiastic graduate students and I was a student in another department who had never even attended a psychology class. But I wrote up a couple of pages of what I was interested in studying and my words touched something in him.

He agreed to be my advisor.

Words can't convey how much Mihaly would influence me. It's rare to have had a mentor who was so highly creative and innovative in his scholarly work. He inspired and supported my passion for pioneering research and exploring unanswerable questions. Together we co-authored an article and book chapters on learning in museums (see *Museum News,* 1995; *The Educational Role of the Museum* edited by Hooper-Greenhill, 1999; *Learning from Museums* by Falk and Dierking, 2000.) I'm deeply grateful for Mike's support, encouragement, and the sturdy foundation he gave me. I learned that I could be both an academic *and* creative. In fact, those parts of myself would blend beautifully.

Looking back, it's easier for me to see the Divine plan. The shaman part of me can open realms of intelligent vibrational energy that lie beyond rational thought, while the scholarly part of me wants to understand these experiences in light of what others have written about learning, knowing, and human consciousness.

The other day a podcast interviewer told me she found my work both fascinating and unnerving. She shared that she'd taken too many drugs when she was younger, which left her with a great fear of losing her mind.

I haven't had that fear. My initial strategy was to dismiss the mystical experiences. But later, the last two shamanic initiations happened while I was teaching at two different graduate schools of psychology. I've always taught courses as if I was a learner along with my students (see my book *Getting Messy* for more on that) and it was clear to me that Spirit intended these shamanic initiations to be part of my course material. In the end, academia—and particularly, depth psychology—gave me a way to own, recognize, and value my encounters with non-ordinary intelligence. It gave me a way to understand non-ordinary experiences in the context of what others had written.

Perhaps you've had your own instances of unexplainable breakthroughs, higher knowing, or extraordinary perception. And perhaps like me, you've dismissed those experiences because you didn't have a place to put them. If so, I hope this book will help you embrace them. The way of knowing that I describe here is an artistic capacity that we humans subconsciously draw upon whenever we're confronted with something that we don't understand but are compelled to try to make sense of.

Ordinary humans have the ability to connect with divine wisdom that lies beyond our thinking mind. We just haven't known how.

When I work with clients and we enter the intelligent field, its power is unmistakable. We know it's alive because *we can feel it.*

Occasionally I sense that a person needs to hear that from me, so I'll speak it out loud: "This is real. You're not making it up." Even though she's experiencing this vibrational energy herself, when I *confirm* to her what is happening, her *being* shifts. The reminder that this dynamic energy is not *of* us cracks open her ordinary perception. She's no longer an isolated soul doing her best to get along in the world.

She's now one with Something greater than herself.

This living field of intelligence can shift and change everything, even human life as we know it. Does that make you pause for a moment?

I ache for it to be known.

Fully developing this way of learning and knowing has massive implications, both for you to live your most authentic life, and for our world.

WHO THIS BOOK IS FOR

In addition to artists, creatives, healers, mystics, and seekers of personal growth, there are others I hope this material speaks to.

SOCIAL CHANGE ACTIVISTS, POLITICIANS, AND POLICYMAKERS

Social activists and policymakers focus their attention on important and complex issues. What matters is *how* those issues are addressed.

Often, when we decide to tackle a problem, an energy dynamic is created: we're on one side and "the problem" is on the other. When we look at the underlying metaphoric pattern, we can see that when we want something to "go away," we make it "bigger" than ourselves. For example, when I look at the metaphoric energy of Covid, it says, "*I need you to shift how you're looking at me, because if you want me to go away, you're attached to me. And when you're attached, you're not in your power.*"

This makes sense, right? When we focus on something outside of ourselves, we make it bigger than us. We give it our power.

In the US, a similar dynamic shows up with local or national issues. Because the United States is so highly polarized, the moment one group stands behind a solution, there automatically arises an equally strong group of people who will fight against it. This is a polarity and in a polarity, no one wins.

We need to open a third space—a place of creative movement that lies *beyond* the polarity.

So for starters, if you're working on something complex, you might notice how free you feel to look at the issue in different, objective, and neutral ways. Are you locked into a side, or attached to a particular way, position, or ideology? This will create a polarity and a polarity will keep you stuck.

Both Carl Jung and Albert Einstein had something insightful to say about solving complex problems. Einstein said that no problem can be solved with the same kind of thinking that created it. And Jung wrote that we don't ever solve complex issues at their own level. Instead, something "higher" or "wider" takes us *beyond* the situation.

I love that. And it's so true, isn't it? Have you had a big issue or concern in your life that magically resolved itself when you saw beyond it? Or *moved* beyond it?

That same logic applies to social change.

Significant social change will happen when we see or move *beyond* our current definitions, frameworks, and thinking.

It's not about the problem. *It's about our ability to see in new ways.*

DIRECTORS OF ORGANIZATIONS, MINISTERS, PRIESTS, LEADERS, AND MEANING-MAKERS

A friend of mine is in her final year of seminary training. Rather than feeling inspired by the new path that lies ahead, she's bored, uninspired, and frustrated. "I'm shocked by the amount of bad preaching. It's like they grab a bunch of shit from their drawers and give it to people," she complained. Her training as a minister has required her to sit through hundreds of sermons and few of them, she says, "cracked open space for the other realm to appear." She sighed, "I hunger to find a place in the world of religion that is life-giving."

Passionate sermons that stir an audience come from a deeper place. Only when we feel the fire of our own inspiration are we able to share that fire with others.

But the task of inspiring others is not just for religious leaders, it's for all who lead groups or organizations. You can get people to do things by creating rules for them to follow or you can *inspire* them to take action. Which organization would you prefer to work for?

By the way, it's not a stretch to say that religious wars happen because metaphoric wisdom is viewed *concretely,* as if it were static. But as you will learn in this book, metaphoric terrain is *creative* ground—it's active, alive, and ever changing. It wants to *move*.

If religious leaders truly understood metaphor, there would be no religious wars.

DOCTORS, NURSES, SOCIAL WORKERS, COUNSELORS, AND ANYONE IN HEALTH OR HEALING PROFESSIONS

Those who've been through a life crisis or serious medical situation know that healing often begins when we discover a sense of meaning in what we're going through. But we can't artificially manufacture meaning—it doesn't come from the intellect.

Meaning comes from a deeper place, a place we don't always have access to.

Relatedly, in therapeutic or medical settings, we may think that a particular counselor or medical professional is "healing" us, but in fact, the healing is coming *through* him or her. The practitioner's skill is intrinsically related to his or her ability to access the power of a realm that lies beyond the thinking mind. One could say that healing happens in a 'third space.'

SCIENTISTS AND ALL THOSE WITH IMPORTANT INFORMATION TO SHARE

I once listened to an interview with a scientist about global warming. He presented all kinds of scientific data about the projected temperatures of the earth and he was adamant: "It's a matter of science, not belief. Scientific research clearly shows that the earth is getting warmer." But when the radio program opened the lines to receive callers, the first caller was unconvinced. Despite this scientist's great effort to explain his carefully collected data, she was unmoved and wouldn't budge from her way of thinking: the earth was *not* getting warmer. The caller reminded me of a friend who had a disagreement with her husband and said, "He can talk until he's blue in the face; he's never going to change my mind."

Scientific data provides us with great information. But unfortunately, *facts do not change beliefs*.

Creative power doesn't come from data, numbers, research, or finely crafted words. It comes from something we can *feel*.

If you have something significant to share, getting your message across often depends less on your expertise or research and more on your talent for connecting with people at a deeper level. Your message needs a way to pierce through our ingrained ideologies and stir something else within us.

TEACHERS, TRAINERS, COACHES, AND MENTORS

Many of us who teach, train, coach, or mentor focus on content and strategies. But more important than content or strategies is your ability to open a rich learning space for your students or clients, ripe with possible new discoveries and unforeseen breakthroughs. Potent creative terrain will take your students well beyond where they thought it was possible for them to go.

No matter what kind of work you do, you have the potential to source it from a realm of profound wisdom and depth. You can offer something inspired, expansive, and generative to your clients, students, colleagues, and community. Who wouldn't want to do that?

ARTISTS, VISIONARIES, AND CREATIVES

I once attended a Christmas Eve service at a small church. The minister told us she was learning to play the harp and would play *Silent Night* for us. As she began to play, it was very apparent that she was a beginner—the song was clunky and she played several wrong notes. Yet her short solo moved me to tears.

I've attended many musical performances in my life and I rarely remember them for their technical proficiency. Technical skill speaks to our heads; something else speaks to our hearts.

At their best, poetry, theater, dance, and other arts *move us*; they *take us somewhere.* We're inspired, renewed, expanded, and shifted into another kind of consciousness. But what *is* that ephemeral thing that moves us? And how do artists tap into it?

If you want to move others with your work, this book will take you deep into your own creative source. And by the way, bravo. I salute your voice, courage, and willingness to explore unknown terrain.

THOSE WHO FEEL STUCK, OVERWHELMED, FRIGHTENED, OR OPPRESSED BY LIMITATION

Nearly all of us experience moments in life when we're stuck or believe we don't have any options. I know a very talented musician who lives in a small town and often complains that there are no places for her to perform. In fact, there are many possibilities for getting her music out into the world, but she can't see them because she has a limited view of what's acceptable. When venues are too small or shabby, they simply aren't on her radar.

Creative power will take you places that aren't realistic or even conceivable. It will bring novel solutions, astonishing healing, and the resolution of long-standing conflicts. Even when you feel stuck or trapped, the creative will find the opening.

THOSE WHO WANT TO DEEPEN THEIR EXPERIENCE OF LIVING IN THIS WORLD

I see so many people spend tens of thousands—and even hundreds of thousands—of dollars on the path that looks rational. The direction that seems most likely to bring the income, relationship, or career success they seek. Others spend oodles of time and money on training programs because they think they need yet another certificate before they do the work they *really* want to do.

But the only trustworthy guidance, the only authentic way to know where and how to focus your energy and resources, is within. Your deep creative terrain has a direction *it* wants to go.

Let's listen to it.

When I was in graduate school, I submitted a paper to one of my professors and his response was, "Is this your best work?" I was embarrassed and said no, it wasn't my best work. So I went home and worked on the paper and brought back a revised version. He again asked me, "Is this your best work?" And once again, I sheepishly said, "... no, I guess not," and re-worked the paper a third time.

This time I was determined to give him my very best. When I brought it back to him, he asked me, "Is this your best work?" I said, "*Yes*, this is my *best* work." He said, "Good. I'll read it now."

PREFACE

This is the third version of this book. For the past ten years, I have wrestled with this material, developing, refining, and clarifying it.

Professor Harlan, I believe this is my best work. You can read this one.

1

UNCOMMON PERCEPTION

When we understand the secret that things are not only as they appear to common sensible perception, we find the need to nurture an uncommon kind of perception.

~ MARY WATKINS

THE FIRST SHAMANIC INITIATION

In the fall of my 26th year, I traveled with my boyfriend to the Upper Peninsula of Michigan to see the autumn colors. Late at night, we were cruising down a country highway at 60+ mph when a car crossed over the center-line and hit us head-on. After the shock of the collision, I tried to get out of the car and could not move my body. I had no sensation below the waist and knew I'd broken my back. I could feel the broken vertebrae. It was the middle of the night in the middle of nowhere. Waiting in the car for the local volunteer paramedics, I tried to remain calm.

When the ambulance that came for me reached the local hospital, the doctor curtly told me not to budge. "This doesn't look good and I can assure you that if you move your body at all, you'll be paralyzed for the rest of your life. Don't move." Then he walked away. So, I lay motionless in the hospital emergency room in excruciating pain, waiting for an air ambulance to take me to a place that could handle spinal cord injuries and patch me back together.

I was scared. My life as I knew it had just ended.

As I lay there in shock and anguish, a nurse came over and whispered in my ear, "Imagine that you're floating on a cloud." I closed my eyes and imagined that I was resting on a soft, feathery cloud. In order to float on this cloud, my body needed to be light, so I focused on *lightness* and I began to relax. After a few moments, the pain became more tolerable and I slowly shifted from a state of trauma into a place of peace.

This experience of floating on a cloud was my first real encounter with the unique power of metaphor to heal and take us to new places. The very real—yet simple—tactile energy of LIGHTNESS sustained me through a night of shock, fear, and suffering. Ultimately, it would heal my body and allow me to walk again.

This was my first shamanic initiation.

The local hospital flew me to one of the best spinal trauma units in the country where doctors said that I had not only broken vertebra, but I had also displaced my spinal cord by 40 degrees. My physician team cautiously gave me a very tiny chance—less than 5%—of being able to walk again and little possibility of ever being able to use my bladder.

After a few days, when the pain began to ease a little and I wasn't spending all my time counting minutes until the next dosage of morphine kicked in, I started to take in what these esteemed physicians were telling me. But despite my sincere desire to understand them, their prognosis never really registered. Even with their impressive credentials and experience, I didn't feel they were giving me a truth. Some part of me knew that I would fully recover from my injuries and walk again.

Why did I not believe them? Why did I have an internal knowing that was different from what the doctors told me? My family greatly valued education and science. My parents and both grandfathers received college degrees in the sciences; my sister is a physician, my brother an engineer. I was young and had never questioned experts, especially revered physicians at a prestigious medical center.

I wasn't feeling resistance toward what these doctors had to say. I wasn't blocking out their words, nor was I trying to do my own thing and prove them wrong. I wasn't locked in a battle with them or the facts they were providing to me. On the contrary, I was open to their thoughts and wanted to learn everything I could from them. What was happening was a knowing on some other level—a level where I could receive their information but make my own decision about what to do with it. This knowing wasn't coming from my rational mind but from someplace that I couldn't see or explain. *I just knew.*

Here's another odd occurrence. Months before the accident, I was a maniac about physical fitness. Every night after work, I played two hours of rigorously competitive racquetball with my male coworkers, followed by a mile lap swim. Although I was young and enjoyed being physically active, that summer I was focused on physical exercise in a way I'd never been before. I had no conscious thought about all this activity. I was simply following some vague inner urging...*as if my body were preparing for something.*

I don't know why my body seemed to know and prepare ahead of time for this significant trauma. I also can't explain why I get frazzled when I have a bad hair day or receive a minor traffic ticket, but when face-to-face with the best physicians in the country telling me that I would be permanently paralyzed from the waist down, I was unfazed. I simply gave no credence to that idea. Sure enough, although the doctors expected me to be in the hospital and rehab center for months, after a few weeks I could walk with the use of a cane and return home. Thirty years later, no one would ever guess the extent of my injuries from that accident.

Not long after, I met a writer who worked in the German Resistance movement during World War II. She was a teenager during the war and she proceeded to tell me story after story of her heroic deeds. The Nazis ultimately captured her along with her partners and while they killed the men she was with, she was spared but subjected to cruel punishment. I asked her, "How could you do it? How could you be so brave?"

She responded, "During war, you're operating on a different level." I was awed by this incredible woman and fascinated by what she said. And despite the drastic differences in our stories, I wondered if perhaps during the time of the accident I was operating on a different level as well.

I didn't know then that the car accident would be the first of three shamanic initiations. Shamanic initiations are spiritual tests where the initiate faces physical or symbolic death. Through these ordeals, they develop skills and capacities for navigating the Spirit world and drawing on it for healing. In each of my initiations, I survived by accessing the intelligent field. Each shamanic initiation taught me something different: how to locate the field, how to enter it, and how to work with its energies.

Just as shamans can enter unseen realms and communicate with animal spirits and totems, I can open a dynamic field of creative intelligence and help my clients enter it as well. My skills for opening this terrain and understanding its language have become finely honed, but I believe we all have this capacity. The earliest humans communicated by sensuously tuning into the natural world around them. They had a natural ability to learn from the wisdom of flowing rivers, thunder, lightning, sunrise, sunset, plant life, and animal life.

This capacity for deep knowing is still with us. We haven't understood how powerful it is.

As I mentioned in the Preface, Spirit didn't choose me for this task because I wanted to be a shaman, nor because my heritage, bloodline, or family lineage led me to it. But perhaps I was shown how to open this realm because my passion in life has been to understand human learning. I'm fascinated by what inspires us to learn and grow. How do we transcend ourselves? How does cultural change happen? These questions have driven my life and work.

In these pages, I share what I've learned from my own surprising experiences with the intelligent field. I've worked in-depth with hundreds of incredibly gifted, creative people in individual sessions and I've spent thirty years teaching a wide array of classes in a broad number of settings—from rigorous graduate programs to community retreat centers. The Psychology of Metaphor class I mention in Chapter 3 provided the original research foundation for this book.

THE POWER OF THE INTELLIGENT FIELD

The intelligent field is what I accessed years ago when I was scared out of my mind on one level, yet firmly aware of inner guidance on another. Many of us endlessly ruminate: *"Is it better for my business if I do this or I do that?"* or *"How do I deal with that annoying neighbor?"* We get stuck thinking in black and white categories: *"Is it A or is it B?"* I want you to know that there's another space of possibility that holds surprising answers that you would never have come up with on your own.

There's a whole other reality.

My clients and I have experienced mystical states, ancient tribal energies, numinous Oneness with the Universe, and creative breakthroughs of all sorts. Spirit guides, Power animals, figures from past lives, ancestors, and sacred energies and gifts may show up during any given session. This vibrational field is three-dimensional— just like things in everyday life. It has terrain, depth, texture, shape, and form. It is shamanic, in that its energies are not OF this world.

Working with this realm will:

- Unleash your creative capacities.
- Restore and strengthen your self-trust.
- Facilitate your connection with Spirit and higher guidance.
- Uncover resources and possibilities that are difficult to access any other way.
- Quickly shift you out of difficulties and into a place of profound beauty, healing, and creative flow.
- Engage potent source energies to improve your relationships, heal your physical body, and accelerate creative breakthroughs.

Visualization is considered by many to be the best way to cure illness, make more money, give an outstanding performance, and so forth. But there's something else that wants to be known and what this book is about—the energetic field in which those images live.

Since the accident, I've learned that the LIGHTNESS energy I experienced was not just a fantasy created by my imagination. There is a realm under the surface that is fully awake and alive, with its own independent intelligence and fierce desire to express itself. This realm of beauty and deep wisdom pulses underneath what otherwise looks ordinary. It can't be perceived through customary ways of looking.

And it desperately wants our attention.

Yet most of us continue to be yanked around by the vagaries and whims of our personalities, belief systems, and very smart intellects that have been molded by cultural norms and ideology.

This approach has gotten us to where we are today.

No matter how much we push, intend, or force our way forward, no matter how committed we are to any given plan, we don't have all the answers we seek. But Something else does.

We humans are brilliant when we allow Something greater to move through us.

When we move beyond our limited ways of thinking and knowing, we have access to genius.

THE ROLE OF METAPHOR

As I mentioned in the Preface, both Carl Jung and Albert Einstein believed that no serious problem is ever solved directly. We don't solve the problem at its own level.

We see beyond it.

Creative breakthroughs happen when we're able to perceive the wisdom that lies beyond our ordinary way of looking.

But what is it, precisely, that takes us to this place beyond??

In his book, *Metaphor Therapy*, psychologist S.B. Kopp wrote that there are three ways in which humans know. With *empirical observation,* we depend on our senses—seeing, touching, smelling, and hearing. The second way is *rational thought*—if something fits logically with what we already know, we accept it as true. But Kopp's third way is *metaphor* and it's not well understood as a form of knowing. When we know something metaphorically, we engage with the transcendent dimension of human experience.

We humans have the capacity to bridge ordinary consciousness into an expansive place where we are at one with Something larger than ourselves. In the film *A Zen Life*, D.T Suzuki shares about an experience of *being* the trees: "I was the same as the trees. It was not that I had ceased to be myself, but I had become the trees as well." This is precisely what metaphor allows us to do. While we stay firmly rooted in the here-and-now, we shift into a vibrational space that bridges human and spirit.

I often describe the vibrational field as under the surface of consciousness, but it might be more accurate to say that we get to it through a shift in our *way of looking*. A shift from perceiving and knowing with our linear, thinking mind to a spatial, artistic way of knowing based in metaphor.

It's likely that when you hear the word metaphor you think of the intellect or a tool of language that poets use. Or perhaps you think of something that's make-believe or not real. But metaphor is a way of knowing and understanding the world. We humans use it whenever we're confronted with something unclear or confusing and grasping for a way to understand our experience: *"I'm in over my head." "I'm going to hold it lightly." "I need to find my center." "I feel like I'm stepping on shattered glass." "That door is open." "I'm holding on too tight." "I'm flowing right now."*

In the field of psychology, metaphor has become increasingly recognized as a helpful tool for uncovering a client's buried feelings, fears, trauma, and the lens through which he views his life and I'm supremely grateful for those who have spread the word about metaphor's therapeutic role. We need a better understanding of it. But this book will take you far beyond metaphor as a cognitive tool.

Working with metaphor in the way that I describe in this book permits us to experience a dimension that we humans have only previously accessed through spontaneous and unplanned visionary experiences. By connecting the human and spiritual, metaphor allows us to enter mystical realms.

Metaphor provides a way into a living field of intelligence and allows us to directly engage with its powerful energies.

RIGHT-BRAIN AND LEFT-BRAIN

Metaphor is the language of the right cerebral hemisphere. In recent years, scientists have noted that the distinction between right-brain and left-brain is overly simplified and that the reality is much more complex. But from the standpoint of someone who studies learning and creativity, I haven't found a better model for distinguishing between two states of consciousness in everyday life—one where we're in flow and connected to Something larger than ourselves and one where we're not.

From my experience going deep into metaphoric patterns with clients, I have found that flow happens when we engage in an artistic, sensual way of knowing that I describe in the following chapters. In this right-brain mode of perception, we have access to a dynamic field of intelligent creative energy that isn't otherwise available to us. This mode of perception appears to operate from a different place than ordinary cognition. I believe it may originate from the heart's energy field, but I will leave that discussion to scientists and others who have researched this area.

SOURCE VIBRATIONS AND DEEP KNOWING

Working with metaphoric images can be strikingly insightful but working with the energies that come through those images has the power to change the world. I call these energies *source vibrations* and to honor them, I've capitalized them in this book. When you come across one, you might take a moment to close your eyes and allow it to move through you. It's *real.*

It's coming from a place that's wiser than all of us.

Source vibrations heal, shift, and transform us. When you're GROUNDED and STURDY, you're more likely to launch that creative work you keep putting off. When your body knows it's safe to REST, you have a place to heal from injury, trauma, and illness. When you experience the STRENGTH and CLARITY of good boundaries, you'll naturally have more satisfying relationships with yourself and with others. When you're INSPIRED like you're on fire, your career is probably exploding as well.

We don't get shifts and breakthroughs by thinking harder or better. Transformation happens when we align with the potent intelligence that lies beyond our rational mind.

To enter the intelligent field, we engage in a way of knowing that I call *deep knowing*. One might also call it non-ordinary knowing, felt sense knowing, or aesthetic knowing, because it involves discerning qualities of beauty and creative movement that lie under the surface. Deep knowing includes our capacity for embodied awareness and intuitive felt sense, our receptivity to beauty and art, and our ability to feel the presence of Something larger than ourselves. I engaged in deep knowing when I experienced the energy of LIGHTNESS flow through my body after the car accident.

Deep knowing is not cognitive. In the intelligent field, there is genuinely nothing to say.

But everything to feel and know.

Deep knowing is not necessarily so strange or radical. Many of us make decisions and navigate through the world in a manner that's intuitive and pre-verbal. Whether it's a career path, a decision about who to marry, or what band to go see on the weekend, we choose the one that feels right—the career that feels inspiring, the house that feels warm and friendly, the partner who brightens our spirits. Real answers don't come from experts, political pundits, or your very wise older brother. They come from the knowing that lies below the surface of your conscious mind.

You can *feel* what is true.

CREATIVE POWER LYING BELOW THE SURFACE

We often define creativity as the process of gathering insights from an existing pool of ideas and then combining those insights in new ways. Many writers also describe creativity as a stretch of intense work followed by an incubation period. Going for a walk, taking a shower, or participating in some other activity that gives us a mental break allows subconscious ideas a chance to pop through. Finally, those of us in the midst of a creative project often think of creativity as something that we tussle with. There's an inner vision that we're trying to "get out" of ourselves and onto the paper, canvas, or dance floor.

From an individual perspective, those are reasonable ways of thinking about creativity, but in this book, I present something very different. My intention is to *shift our focus* from a narrow, self-centered view of creativity to a vast realm of intelligent energy.

Creativity is not just a personal tool for our projects. It's an alignment with a greater intelligence.

One could call this realm the *imagination*, but that word has a bad reputation in our culture. Our contemporary view of the imagination is that it's fairy tale make believe—kind of like the cartoon characters at Disneyland. We scold our child: "*That's nonsense, it's just your imagination,*" or "*You're just imagining that,*" meaning that he or she is making it up, and therefore, it's not true. Even metaphor has that connotation. When people say, "That's just a metaphor," they mean it's not real.

But what I'm talking about is very real.

This realm is about our creative capacities, but creativity is viewed as lightweight fluff by most of the world. We think of creativity as playtime, an activity we do for fun with friends or that children engage with in art classes. And on the other end of the spectrum, creativity is considered something that only professional artists do when they're sequestered away in their studios.

Creativity has not been given its due respect as the driving force behind our growth, happiness, vitality, and success.

The truth of the matter is this: *Creativity is how change happens*. It's the energy that moves us forward in life.

I can't think of anything more powerful than that.

You've likely experienced days of feeling like you're part of some larger creative flow: you get the parking spot right when you need it, you discover you're overbooked but then a client calls to cancel, your holiday vacation comes together magically, your husband gets the job of his dreams. Things are finally *working* and you're feeling on top of the world.

You probably also know what it feels like to be stuck like you're slogging through muck. Things are just *not happening*. Something is missing, something you can't put your finger on. Or everything's going wrong: the moment your business finally starts taking off, you break your ankle; you meet the man you've fantasized about for years but lose his number. It's just *so frustrating*.

Well, why does that happen?? What causes us to be aligned and in flow? And how can we get those breakthroughs when we need them?

The writer Margaret Silf wrote: *"Ultimately, all the firepower that the world can muster is not capable of pushing a single crocus through the frozen winter soil."* We all live in not one world, but two: the physical world we can see and a realm of creative intelligence that we can't see.

When vibrational energy moves through us—bringing inspiration, answers, flow, and miracles—the potency of this realm is abundantly clear.

Creative power is everything.

Our lives are in a state of constant growth, fueled by dynamic creative energies. Engaging these energies gives us the remarkable ability to transform things that aren't serving us. From resolving relationship difficulties to galvanizing a stagnating career to healing depression, anxiety, and physical ailments. On a global scale, complex and troublesome organizational and social issues are ripe territory for a fresh perspective and creative breakthroughs.

Consciously working with the powerful creative energies of the intelligent field will transform our world.

KEYS TO DEEP KNOWING

An intelligent field of energy pulses underneath what otherwise looks ordinary.

Creative breakthroughs happen when we perceive what lies beyond our ordinary way of looking.

We access the intelligent field when we shift from looking with our analytical mind to an artistic, sensual way of knowing based in metaphor.

Creativity is not just a personal tool for our projects. It is an alignment with a greater intelligence.

PARADIGM SHIFT

The true work of the mind is to reconnect us with that which would otherwise be out of reach.

~ *PARKER PALMER*

BLACK OOZE.

A few years ago, I had a gruesome vision. I found myself in a dark cave, and as my eyes grew accustomed to the dark, I realized I was surrounded by millions of women's bodies whose heads had been cut off. It was unspeakably grisly—the women's bodies hung like silent ghosts, while the rope that was used to bind them lay next to me on a stool. In the dark, eerie quiet, I felt I was in the presence of all the women throughout history who had been physically silenced.

I approached this vision using the methods that I share in this book: I *became* the millions of women's headless bodies. And as the headless bodies, it was clear that I had no voice. I had no power to speak or do anything that normal humans could do.

But what was incredible was, *I was not stuck.*

There was something I could do; there was a *way* I could move—*I could melt.* So, I melted and became thick black ooze.

The ooze had a tremendous amount of energy and it wanted to *go*, so I allowed the movement to happen, and the ooze immediately moved out in every possible direction. When I/it tried to cross over bridges or thresholds, heavy barricades and walls slammed down in front of me. This black ooze was not welcome in any system of authority in the world.

I was being shut out, *but that did not matter.*

Heavy walls could not stop me because I was not a solid substance—*I was fluid.* I could ooze into cracks and crevices, quickly finding any available opening. I continued and covered everything in my path—walls, buildings, roads, bridges, oceans, trees, and rivers. Finally, when the thick black ooze had buried everything on earth and nothing was left except blackness, the vision abruptly ended.

At first, the vision left me shaken. I had just experienced the complete destruction of planet earth. But the energetic vibration, the sensuous *feeling quality* of the black ooze was far from horrific. Yes, it was fierce and destructive, but it was also very much alive and awake.

One might think that as headless bodies, I would be powerless. But when I moved out of my thinking and into deep knowing, *I experienced tremendous power*. Blocked doors and other *obstacles were of absolutely no consequence*. I could ooze under and over and around and through *anything*.

Nothing of this world could stop me.

We could easily assign all kinds of meaning to this vision and many might immediately conclude that it's about female oppression and patriarchy. But we're not working with ordinary knowing. For me, it was the *unrelenting force* of the black ooze—its tremendous and fierce determination— that seeped its way into my psyche and changed my life. That unstoppable, ferocious energy is still working me, teaching me, and moving through me.

Fierce black ooze wrote this book.

In the following chapters, you will awaken a way of knowing that will allow you to tap this fierce, otherworldly intelligence for guidance, healing, inner peace, and breakthroughs.

A PARADIGM SHIFT

For as long as humans have been on this earth, we've been engaging with the imagination. Humans have been accessing inner images since pre-historic times when tribes painted visions onto cave walls. Going on inner journeys is an ancient practice.

So, it's not surprising that throughout history there have been many great teachers. Some of you may relate the concepts in this book with your training in voice dialogue, art therapy, guided visualization, focusing, or dream analysis, to name just a few. Others may see connections with Gestalt therapy, somatic psychology, family constellations, phenomenology, or the telling of myths, poems, and stories. Carl Jung called his work active imagination, James Hillman used the term archetype, and there is a growing field of psychotherapy called metaphor therapy. These are all valid techniques that many people, including myself, have found helpful and healing.

But while those are all popular and effective modalities, I would like to make some clear distinctions, because the work that I present in this book wasn't developed from an existing form of imagery work or technique.

In many image-based psychotherapy methods, the focus is on coming up with associations: *What does this image—house, witch, galaxy of stars, turkey—mean to me?* We see an image of a sun and decide it means we need to shine more at our job. We see a road and interpret it to mean we should take a trip. We see a house and think it means we need to move.

Relatedly, we also assign values to these images: a castle is good, a tumbleweed is bad, a snake is either good or bad depending on your religious upbringing, and so on. Associations and values come from how we *think*—we perceive the image through the lens of our belief systems.

The image gets reduced to us—our current ideology and stance on the world.

But consider that when we're stuck, it's usually because of how we're *thinking* about something. So, if we let our analytical mind interpret an image, we're still in stuckness. We're firmly within the parameters of what we already know.

There's no movement into Something else.

I'd like to introduce you to a paradigm shift. We need a way to move *out* of our rational mind to work with Something larger than ourselves, because like the story of the black ooze demonstrates...

It's not about being in control.

LAYOUT OF THE BOOK

In the next chapter, I briefly review conventional views of learning and creativity, along with my sense that something was missing in our understanding of these human processes. At the end of the chapter, I share my own breakthrough journey into mystical realms and the shamanic initiation where Spirit laid bare this powerfully beautiful realm and asked me to reclaim our human access to it.

Chapter 4 introduces the power of metaphor and how it allows us to engage in intimate dialogue with our animate world. Along with a new way of knowing comes a shift in what we perceive and in Chapter 5, I describe how we humans see certain things and don't see other things. I also introduce the core concept of deep knowing: the sensual and aesthetic language that operates independently of our thinking mind and is common throughout all cultures. In Chapters

6 through 8, I introduce my work with clients and demonstrate how metaphoric images open spaces that we can't get to any other way. And in Chapter 9, I share how deep knowing is a way of *being* and review its most important aspects. Throughout these chapters, I offer stories and examples that will allow you to feel the subtle energy of the intelligent field.

Sprinkled throughout are exercises that will help you develop deep knowing and get a sense of it working in your life. As your channel for deep knowing begins to open, something in you will quicken, initiating breakthroughs and shifts.

There are different ways you can engage with this material and various levels at which you can approach it, so let your intuition guide you. Since we're working with a field of energy, it's best to allow the material to 'work you' and see what shows up. When we open the intelligent field, we can never know what it will bring. Answers will be surprising and come in roundabout ways. Some breakthroughs will be quick and immediate; others will open places inside yourself that you'll spend a lifetime growing into.

By the way, I don't mean to disparage our thinking—of course, we need it to live in this world. But as a culture that's going through upheaval and addressing daunting issues such as global climate change and the rise of extremism, I would argue that we need *all* of our ways of knowing at our disposal.

Embracing another way of knowing is tricky. We must unhook from our fixed ways of looking, our impatience, and the demands we put on ourselves long enough to glimpse something else. When we loosen our automatic responses to what we think and believe (when we give our weary brain a rest), we allow another way of knowing to emerge.

This way of knowing isn't cognitive and it helps when I remind my clients of that.

So, as you read this book, you might occasionally tell yourself: *"This is not cognitive. This is another way."* Then pause for a couple moments and see if you can feel a shift.

It's there.

ON ANOTHER NOTE

My primary intent is to describe and teach another way of knowing, not to write a book about spirituality. So, for those of you who aren't spiritually oriented, I encourage you to continue reading. You don't have to believe in the Divine or mystical realms for this book to shift you. You must merely be curious about what lies beyond what you know.

Information, guidance, breakthroughs, and insights often come to us in non-verbal and non-rational ways. And because of that, we tend to dismiss them.

What have *you* dismissed?

I hope that my journey to understand and clarify my own experiences of non-ordinary knowing and otherworldly connections will inspire you to acknowledge and honor your own. There's something below the surface that wants your attention.

I want you to discover it.

SAFE TRAVELS

In all my years of doing this work, I have never had a client who received anything scary or frightening from the intelligent field. It wants to *help* us. However, sometimes people come to this work with PTSD or something that's really scaring them, or perhaps they've been spooked by an image they received from a night dream. If you can't shake a troubling image, please start with Awakening Deep Knowing exercises #5 and #6, and I also suggest reading Chapter 6. Whenever we address something that's unsettling, we need to open nurturing, loving space for ourselves and those

three things will help you do that. If they don't shift you into a peaceful state, please see a trained counselor.

KEYS TO DEEP KNOWING

Associations and values come from how we *think*—we perceive the image through the lens of our belief systems. *The image gets reduced to us—our current stance on the world.*

When we're stuck it's usually because of how we're thinking about something. So, when we interpret an image, we're still in stuckness.

We need a way to move *out* of our rational mind to work with Something larger than ourselves.

When we loosen our automatic responses to what we think and believe (when we give our weary brain a rest), we allow another way of knowing to emerge.

AWAKENING DEEP KNOWING #1

CHERISHED IMAGES FROM CHILDHOOD

Our personal mythic reality—our own metaphoric structure of individual reality—is revealed in our early memory metaphors.

Richard Kopp, METAPHOR THERAPY

Under the surface of your conscious mind, there's a primary metaphoric image that's feeding your life and shaping how you see. These primary images come from happy memories that were imprinted on your heart when you were a child. They come from things, situations or people that you cherished and they're often associated with the natural world.

Your primary image could be a memory of your home's physical terrain (backyard, a favorite tree, mountains, natural bodies of water). It could be an object from your parents' lives or occupations (your mother's stethoscope, your father's briefcase). It could be a scene such as cooking in your grandmother's kitchen or fishing with your dad. One of my students who grew up in Mexico holds the image of festive local markets in her heart. Their color, vibrancy, and lively people have guided her and given her life meaning. The writer E.B. White was fascinated by spider webs as a child. He went on to write the bestselling book, *Charlotte's Web*.

The image that has guided my own life is my father and grandfather digging in soil and planting in the fields. Despite having lived nearly all my adult life in the city, rich soil is my place of inner nourishment and strength. When I feel lost or in despair, nurturing soil is what brings me back to my center. This simple, sensory metaphor has guided and inspired me throughout my entire life.

Try this...

When you think about your childhood, what images come to mind? What people, places, and things do you remember fondly? Of those images, what one feels like a *support*—something you can rest or settle into? Does it move you emotionally when you reflect on it?

Once you have your image, ask yourself:

- How has this image shaped how I see the world and my place in it?

- How does it help me understand the events of my life?
- How does it nurture and support me when life is difficult?
- What guidance does it offer my future?
- *If this image could speak directly to me, what would it say?*

When a career coach did this exercise, she said it was deeply meaningful and helped her understand her 'ramshackle' life:

> *I keep going back to this country house we had. I always call it "ramshackle magic." It was one of the first experiences I ever had that became the basis of my whole life. Because we had a nice house in Brooklyn, a more respectable house that had higher value than this place. But I wasn't happy in the Brooklyn house, I was happy in the ramshackle house. Your exercise helped me realize, "Wow, what was valuable to the world wasn't necessarily valuable to me." That image explains so much to me. It tells me how my life's work makes sense.*

Potent metaphoric images help us understand our own unique ways of perceiving the world. They are gifts, not only for ourselves, but for others.

3

BEYOND LOGICAL REASONING

I give you the end of a golden string...

it will lead you in at Heaven's gate.

~ WILLIAM BLAKE

CREATIVITY ISN'T LOGICAL.

I once waited for a plane at an airport with a young scientist who had just won a fellowship for his work with creativity in science. When I asked him for an example of scientific creativity, he responded, "How does the sky become blue?" which led me to question, "Why does the sky have to be *blue*?"

Creativity has had a problematic history in our culture because we naturally want to approach it as we do any other strategic problem: *logically*. In a way our brilliant brains can understand, control, and manage.

Starting with the endpoint of "the sky is blue" limits our creative options and possibilities. Think of Claude Monet's Impressionist paintings. Monet didn't look at snow and say, "Hmmm. Snow is white, so how should I paint it?" We engage in creativity when we explore something with openness, without a predefined idea of what we're engaging in or looking at. Snow isn't necessarily white and the sky doesn't have to be blue.

I felt a kinship with the young scientist because I have my own experience of trying to fit an expansive human gift into a logical frame. At the time of the car accident described in Chapter 1, I worked as a computer scientist for a company that produced custom-built semi-trucks. My team was tasked with creating an expert system that would replace the in-house engineers. But I soon came to realize that there was no way a machine could fully replace our most extraordinary human capacity: creativity.

A computer *can* come up with something innovative by generating iterative sets of random possibilities. In other words, if it churns out a lot of stuff, *something* will spark some ideas. The computer's attempts at creativity remind me of brainstorming sessions, which have the same sort of flavor. When we brainstorm, we use our thinking minds to generate endless possibilities. But what we're really doing is firing off a bunch of drivel to see if anything will stick.

Your intellect can come up with all kinds of ideas, but your knack for producing them is not necessarily healing or helpful. Just ask any wildly creative person who has *way* more ideas than he can execute. Or a new business owner overwhelmed with all the things she should do to market her business. Or witness the rapid spread of far-out conspiracy theories. Many psychologists would claim that stress comes from this kind of runaway imagination.

There's a distinct difference between our mind's ability to generate ideas and genuine creative breakthroughs.

The greatest inventors and creators did not come up with new insights through iterative processes such as brainstorming. A truly creative solution comes from a different way of knowing. For lack of a better description, we often call these moments "flashes of insight."

WANTING SOMETHING MORE

When I was a Ph.D. student, I couldn't wait to dive into the research on human learning. By this time, I had experienced my first shamanic initiation and other spontaneous episodes of being one with an expanded Divine consciousness. I wanted to understand my experiences.

Through my research, I discovered that human learning is often defined as a process of taking action and then reflecting on the results. We make plans, experiment, observe the outcome, and incorporate our findings into a new plan. Although I use this method of learning, on its own it felt rote, mechanical, and unsatisfying. It was describing something that a computer could do. This framework couldn't explain moments of mystery, intuition, synchronicity, or higher vision. It couldn't help me understand my gut knowing at the time of the accident or tell me how the energy of black ooze wrote this book. It couldn't explain breakthroughs, leaps in consciousness, or unexpected encounters with a living intelligence that wasn't my own.

Standard definitions of human learning lacked beauty, mystery, and grace. They lacked messiness, surprise, and unexpected leaps.

I knew there must be something more.

Learning and creativity are inherently intertwined. Learning is how we perceive the world, comprehend our lives, and make meaning. Creativity is how we live—it's what we do with what we know. If you have a narrow perception of the world, you'll have a narrow perception of what is possible. What we think and believe defines the boundaries of our creativity.

How we perceive determines every action we take.

To my mind, we need an expanded model of human learning that supports—and even inspires—breakthroughs.

AWAKENING ANOTHER WAY OF KNOWING

After I finished my Ph.D., I needed a mental break. For years I'd stuffed words inside my head; now they swam in front of me and made me nauseous. When a friend suggested I take a class at the Berkeley Psychic Institute, I swiftly agreed. It sounded fun and offbeat.

It was a total lark.

The poet William Blake said that if we follow the golden string it will lead us to Heaven's Gate and the class at Berkeley Psychic Institute ended up being a golden string. When I gave someone a 'psychic reading,' I noticed that I wasn't predicting his or her future. Instead, I found myself dropping down to a level where I read the person's metaphoric patterns. I could see her slogging through muck, or needing to set a boundary, or yearning for a break, or dealing with something that was hanging over her head. I could see a person's frustration because he was fervently trying to open a door that was never going to open.

I saw the many ways in which we humans limit ourselves.

Everything I saw was a metaphor.

Seeing metaphoric images was interesting to me. Doing these readings, I had access to a new kind of language that I could read just as quickly as I could read words. This language was merely coming from another place.

But eventually, I tucked my experience away and moved on to more sensible things.

Twelve years later, I spoke to the president of a graduate school of psychology about teaching in his Ph.D. program. I didn't have any predefined ideas about what I wanted to teach at this school, but I presumed it would be related to teaching and learning. In the interview, he looked at me quizzically and then said, "Instead of trying to fit you into our program, why don't you tell me what you'd like to teach."

What happened next would change the course of my life. A voice spoke through me and said, "Metaphor."

He said, "Great! We'll call it the Psychology of Metaphor" and I was stunned. I didn't know anything about metaphor as an academic subject, nor how it related to psychology. I walked out of there wondering how I would pull this off. In a few short weeks I would be teaching this course to a bunch of Ph.D. students.

Astonishing synchronicities showed up almost immediately. Soon after our conversation, old, out-of-print books about metaphor and its influence on how we think and learn appeared in improbable ways. For example, while sitting at a table in the library, I would glance up from what I was reading. Lying there in front of me would be yet another obscure book about metaphor waiting patiently for me to notice it.

I swear it wasn't there when I sat down.

These books rocked my world. It was as if the world had forgotten these texts and Spirit had tasked me with rediscovering them. One of the most impressive was *Symbol and Metaphor in Human Experience,* published in 1949 by a long-forgotten philosopher named Martin Foss. Foss's work spoke to me on a deep level. For Foss, metaphor is not merely a tool for our rational minds to play with: it is *life itself.*

Metaphor is the creative process of life.

Other writers that inspired me were Gregory Bateson, depth psychologist Robert Romanyshyn, philosophers Henry Corbin and David Abram, and of course, George Lakoff and his fifty years of exceptional scholarship on metaphor and embodied cognition. I also read with interest authors who had expertise on right-brain processes such as Betty Edwards, Jerome Bruner, Leonard Shlain, Jill Bolte Taylor, and Bob Samples, among others.

Finally, research on synesthesia intrigued me. Synesthesia happens when a person sees numbers or words as colors, shapes, or textures. To my mind, the implications of synesthesia are profound: if *some* of us can experience words or numbers in sensory and aesthetic ways, it means that this ability is likely *available* to all of us. Synesthesia also confirmed that there *is* an intelligent aesthetic realm under the surface and we humans have the capacity to plug into it.

A SECOND SHAMANIC INITIATION.

These fascinating books awakened something in me and altered the way I saw the world. Taken together, they suggested a realm of profound beauty and wisdom that we humans can't access through ordinary ways of knowing.

I developed a strong desire to experience this beauty and madly searched for a "way in." Every day, gazing at the world around me, I whispered to any Divine messengers that might be listening, "*How do I see the beauty? How do I see the beauty?*" There was something under the surface and I wanted to see it.

But I had no idea how.

Two months later, as if in response to my request, Spirit lifted the veil. I was gripped by a visionary experience that would change my life forever. Plucked from an ordinary state of consciousness one evening, Spirit showed me the striking, otherworldly beauty that I'd sensed and yearned for in the metaphor class.

This divine beauty was pulsing and glorious, and vibrated from everything around me—trees, plants, sky, animals.

It was the beauty I'd yearned for, and it took my breath away.

While I gazed in stunned wonder, I was suddenly yanked up into the air and pummeled at high speed through the sky. As I was sped toward a distant mountain, I realized that I was going to slam into it and die.

I had no choice. Something had me firmly in its grip. I braced myself for instant pulverization.

But at the very last second, I was yanked into a train tunnel going through the mountain. I looked out the train window and witnessed once again the exquisite, otherworldly beauty. The moment I saw the beauty, a voice said, "THIRD SPACE" and I bolted back into ordinary reality.

This was my second shamanic initiation.

This time, I couldn't dismiss my experience and move on. I had just faced instant death. Yet dramatically rescued at the very last second.

Something was trying to communicate with me. Urgently.

Third space was a concept that I taught in my class and wrote about in my book, *Getting Messy*. The term originally came to me by way of Charles Johnston, a psychologist and expert on creativity who used it to refer to the creative state that occurs when a polarity is bridged. In my work, I've expanded Johnston's definition of third space to include a place of inner vision and inner knowing where we're connected with Divine wisdom. Third space is the place where we're aligned and hooked up to the guidance of the intelligent field.

But *why* did Spirit show me third space in such a forceful way? What was I supposed to *do* with this fiery communication from Spirit?

Spirit was demanding that I *act*. But.... *how*?

It haunted me.

THIRD SPACE

Even if done more carefully, diligently, or skillfully, logical thinking was no match for the visceral force of this encounter. I simply wasn't going to understand it—or know what to do next—through reasoning or logic.

A couple of months later, I read this sentence in *The Authentic Dissertation*, a book by Trent Jacobs, a Native American and professor at Fielding Graduate University: "Vision is considered to be a legitimate source for new knowledge in Indigenous cultures and vision was the centerpiece of my own dissertation."

The author Parker Palmer uses the phrase "divided no more" to name the point at which we can no longer live in disharmony within ourselves. Trent Jacobs' assertion that visions are a vital way of knowing... struck me.

There is more to human learning than we know or acknowledge.

I once heard the acclaimed filmmaker David Lynch interviewed on the NPR program *Fresh Air*. When host Terry Gross asked him about what he does when he makes a movie, Lynch paused for a moment and then responded, "Terry, when I'm making a movie, I don't really know what I'm doing." He had no answer for her. Of course, there was *something* that was guiding his work, but whatever it was, wasn't something he could verbalize.

Perhaps his process looks like this: *Does this action feel right? Is this piece flowing today? What is missing? What might happen if I tried this?* He experiments, investigates patterns, and gathers bits of ideas together until the project starts to jell into a form. He engages a deeper way of knowing, led by a vision that only he can see. This vision isn't something he perceives in the physical world, nor is it an entirely *inner* one. It lies somewhere in-between his inner and outer world.

His vision lies in a third space.

A spider weaves its web and then waits for its prey to come. Our traditional ways of thinking and knowing are like being stuck inside the spider's web. We can think and think and try and try, but there is still no way out of the web. And whenever we think we know, we get even more mired in the maze.

When we confine our knowing to logical thought, we stay stuck inside the spider's web. It's a severe misperception to believe that if we just try hard enough, we'll get somewhere new.

We won't.

But when we soften our resistance and rest down into a more ancient, innate, felt sense way of knowing, we're able to discern a realm that lies beyond the spider's web. That's what we'll be doing in this book.

KEYS TO DEEP KNOWING

If you have a narrow perception of the world, you'll have a narrow perception of what is possible for you and those around you.

There's a distinct difference between our mind's ability to generate ideas and genuine creative breakthroughs.

Something guides us that we can't verbalize.

Information, guidance, breakthroughs, and insights often come to us in non-verbal and non-rational ways. And because of that, we dismiss them.

AWAKENING DEEP KNOWING #2

THE METAPHORIC BEAUTY OF PLACES, PEOPLE, AND THINGS.

A few years ago, I was in a band that regularly played at seedy bars (one place was famous for a grisly murder). But despite the shabby venues, it was pure magic when a room full of scruffy strangers lit up in song and dance.

Magic isn't the product of experts, finesse, polish, or hype. Magic happens when we allow ourselves to drop down to the beauty that lies under the surface.

You can go to a redwood forest or a desert to soak up the earth's artistry, but just for today, I challenge you to discover beauty in an unexpected place or situation. I once heard someone say that beauty is the depth at which we see something. You might take a moment to notice something special about a random situation, person, or thing—something that the rest of us might overlook.

Spend a day keeping your eyes—and your heart—open. Write down those moments of unexpected beauty. Share them with somebody or bring them into a creative project you're working on. Beauty is meant to be shared.

ENGAGING AN ANIMATE WORLD

[An animate world] opens the possibility of interaction and exchange, allowing reciprocity to begin to circulate.

~ DAVID ABRAM, *Becoming Animal*

ARTISTS TOUCH WHAT IS ALIVE

Sigmund Freud is credited as saying that no matter where his research led, a poet had already been there ahead of him. And the physicist Arthur Zajonc said, "We now truly stand in need, not only as scientists but as a civilization, of the artist's cognitive capacities."

The question is, *why*? What is it that poets and artists do that take them beyond ordinary capacities for learning and knowing?

Perhaps it's the artist's willingness to be confused, welcoming any unlikely connection that shows up; or his or her sensitivity to nuance and qualities of beauty that others miss. Perhaps artists are more flexible and disposed to "go with the flow." Maybe they are more comfortable with risk-taking and are more inclined to let curiosity lead the way.

I grew up in a hardworking Norwegian farming family and Midwestern practicality is etched into my cells. When I walk into an art gallery, I often marvel at the amount of time someone spent gluing hundreds of tiny pieces of glass into a sculpture or creating a fine painting. Thousands of hours in many cases, with no practical benefit other than to be looked at and admired. We can look at and admire a tree or a bouquet of flowers. Why do we need art?

We tend to evaluate the success of artists by whether they earn an income selling their work. This is not an easy path and for many artists it's a struggle. But perhaps there are other reasons why artists labor against the odds to produce art. Maybe underneath it all, it's not so much about making pretty things for people to look at and buy.

Perhaps what they do—consciously or not—is engage in a process that lets them *touch something that's alive.* Maybe their creative efforts help the rest of us touch that place as well.

Maybe by allowing us to engage with Something more expansive than ourselves, the creative process teaches us how to be better humans.

YOU ARE NOT ALONE IN THIS WORLD

I once sat on a stool in an international retreat center's art studio painting a paper-mache mask. I'd initially signed up for some sort of contemplative workshop but found it too cerebral and ended up here.

I painted the mask magenta and then decided to paint a vine on one side. As I slowly drew a long vine down the side of my mask—getting into the feeling of the vine's graceful, elegant beauty—*Something drew with me.*

I was no longer directing my hand, Something else was. Something else was carrying me, stroking the paint on this mask.

Some sort of divine life force beyond what I could know or understand was moving my hand.

Painters, dancers, sculptors, musicians, and artists throughout history have often said that their creative visions were not *of them,* so I know I'm not the only one who has experienced the movement of otherworldly creative energy. To write that beautiful poem, or dance that exquisite dance, or make art that touches and transforms, artists partner with Something greater than themselves.

The creative process puts us in touch with transcendent energies.

Being moved by Divine creative energies is uplifting and exquisitely beautiful, like nothing else I have ever experienced. Yet, these unique experiences have primarily remained in the province of mystics and artists.

So why are they important for the rest of us?

I don't know about you, but here's what's been true for me. So much of my life has been about struggle and effort. I pushed and tried so hard, beat myself up when I made mistakes, and bore the weight of too much fear and worry on my shoulders. When I had distressing thoughts, I assumed those thoughts were real. I soldiered on, making all kinds of plans and commitments, believing that I was solely in charge of my destiny. When I was stressed, overwhelmed, or things weren't going well, I thought what I was experiencing was absolute.

But then I discovered another way of knowing that shifts me into a place of expansiveness and freedom—from myself *and* my problems. A place of *being* rather than *doing*, a place where I am bigger than I think I am, a place where my physical body can rest and heal. It's a place where I receive insight and direction, strengthen my voice and confidence, get clarity, have more satisfying and loving relationships, realize my highest creative potential, and delight in possibilities I would never imagine.

It's a place I can trust.

Transformative change doesn't come from solitary struggle; it comes from partnering with the powers that lie under the surface. *That* is when we're brilliant.

There's an unseen dimension that very much wants to work with us. Its aim is not to eliminate labor from our lives nor make everything fun, light, and easy. (I'm sure that Joan of Arc and Martin Luther King felt overwhelmed and challenged at times.) There will be times when you need to rest, let go, or allow yourself to be heavy with sadness. There will be times when you need to buckle down and put your nose to the grindstone. But it's all in service to a larger creative flow.

You are not alone in this world. An intelligent field of energy wants to support you.

METAPHOR TAKES YOU SOMEWHERE

In *Spirited Leading and Learning,* Peter Vaill said that the essential starting point of artistic consciousness is acknowledging that something is "*more than I can possibly know.*" When we admit that we don't know everything, we have to *feel* our way to understanding, gathering little bits and pieces together until things start to jell and we gain more clarity. So, to help us find our way through this mysterious terrain where we can't see or know for sure, let's dive more deeply into metaphor. After all, it's what catalyzed my journey.

Metaphor operates below our conscious minds. It's not something we can understand through a rational thinking process. It's not quite of this world; it seems to be in-between the realms and trying to define it is slippery. In fact, in *Death, Sacrifice and Tragedy,* Martin Foss goes so far as to say metaphor is "the secret of all life. It is the innermost secret of the life of God himself."

Wow. That's sort of a big thing to ponder.

We are poised at the brink of something that seems enormous and unwieldy, something that is bigger than our minds can fully understand. So, we can just start with the basics.

An example of a *simile* is this: "Ted is *like* a wolf." On the other hand, a *metaphorical* statement would be: "Ted *is* a wolf." The sentence "Ted is like a wolf," is literal, linear. It doesn't take us anywhere new. We have Ted on the one hand and we have a wolf on the other, and we can compare the qualities of each to see what is alike. Similes are like the computer's attempts at creativity that I described in Chapter 2. We have not entered new terrain and our brains have not been stretched. We are still firmly planted within our own narrow definition of reality.

Metaphor, on the other hand, doesn't make logical sense. When we hear the phrase, Ted *is* a wolf, our rational mind screams out, "Whoa@%^&*! That's not true! Ted is *not* a wolf!" And then this logical part of our brain quickly gives up, becoming exasperated with anything that doesn't fit its model of the world. At which point our imaginations come into action and are quite happy to engage in this conversation. At the moment our linear minds give up, we enter a new place where another kind of wisdom lives.

Something shifts and suddenly, Ted looks different to us. He has new energy, a unique quality that we hadn't seen before. In *The Everyday Work of Art,* Eric Booth writes, "In metaphor, we enter new worlds of the possible." Suddenly, we've stepped into a realm where the statement "Ted is a wolf" is, astonishingly, *TRUE.*

Metaphor *opens up a space* where there is no problem with Ted being a wolf. Ordinary language has somehow dissolved the separation between two entirely dissimilar things to create something new. How powerful is *that*?

Through our capacity for metaphor, we can open spaces that in a logical world *do not exist.*

Whereas an image gives you something to look at and analyze, a metaphor gives you an experience. *It takes you somewhere.*

EMBRACING A SENSUAL WAY OF KNOWING

I have a client who is a professional dancer. Her gift is sensuality and the metaphoric image that often shows up in our sessions is of a beautiful, sensual snake slowly winding its way around and up the trunk of a tree.

Take a moment to close your eyes and imagine you *are* the snake. You are fully embodied, fully whole, thoroughly enjoying slithering your beautiful body seductively around this tree trunk. You are fully in-the-moment and present to your bodily experience. As you move in your beautifully graceful way, you appreciate the firmness and strength of the trunk, the roughness of the bark.

Can you feel the beautiful sensuality here? That's *real energy.*

I offer this example because I believe our human connection with Spirit operates in a similarly sensual way. While our left hemisphere responds to the world in a rational, logical, analytical, and distant way, our right hemisphere responds sensually. It wants intimacy, feeling, connection, and relationship. That's how it learns.

We all have an innate capacity to have an intimate, sensual relationship with Something greater than ourselves.

Who doesn't want that?

By the way, I spent a bit of time researching the words *sensual, sensory,* and *sensuous* to make sure I accurately portrayed this partnership with Spirit. Sensory is "of the senses" and sensuous is traditionally defined as "appealing to the senses." Both words help distinguish deep knowing from the intellect, so I've used those terms when appropriate in this book.

However, while it makes sense to think of deep knowing as sensory and sensuous, it's also more than that. We're not engaging with the world in the usual way.

We're going to a realm where *feeling* is the only learning capacity we'll have available to us.

I love the word sensual because it *is* erotic and evocative—it's about fully feeling something. That's what we do when we make love, right? We feel our way with the other person. Sometimes that feeling is soft and gentle, sometimes light, sometimes heavy, sometimes hard. Sometimes confusing, sometimes empty. We notice the quality of the touch we're receiving and we respond to it.

That's what we're doing here. *We're feeling our way. We're noticing the quality that's present and letting that quality move us.*

Simple. And profound.

ALIVE WITH CREATIVE POSSIBILITY

We've covered a lot of ground. Let's breathe for a moment and collect our thoughts. Something is pulsing beneath the surface. We have ancient ways of knowing that have been forgotten. The world is animate. Metaphor carries us to new places.

Simultaneously, at once, metaphor is a language, a way of seeing, a way of knowing, a sixth sense, a movement from one reality to another, and a language that—according to the psychologist James Hillman—provides us the ability to communicate with our souls. For Bateson, metaphor is the organizing glue of the world of mental process, and for Foss, the innermost secret of God himself.

Metaphor seems to be everything simultaneously: an image, a process, a bridge, another dimension, the language of the heart, a glue that holds the world together, a thinking apparatus, and the secret of God. Metaphors aren't just a way to *describe* our experience; they directly *create* new experiences.

Metaphor gives us a way to enter a third space.

Of all these definitions, we commonly think of metaphor as a BRIDGE and it *does* act as a bridge. It takes us somewhere new and connects diverse things. It's a path of connection, a vehicle or way to traverse from one realm to another. But metaphor seems to be much more than that; it appears to be *bigger* than that. So, we'll take a moment to explore it experientially.

When I "feel into" metaphor as a BRIDGE, I feel tight and constricted...not expansive. In Awakening Deep Knowing #9 I suggest writing as your image. When I write as the bridge, I got this message: *"I am the bridge. I'm way too tight. You can't unroll me. I'm trapped potential. I only know myself in my world—others don't know me. I'm stuck space, trapped space."*

The feeling of tightness makes sense—bridges have to be rigid and fixed to support us.

When I ask my deep knowing for a more appropriate metaphor for metaphor, what emerges is a CAULDRON OF STEW. Its message is: *"I am metaphor. I have a creative flux and flow inside me like a cauldron—a stew where all kinds of interesting ingredients can be mixed in. Some ingredients keep their form; some blend in. I don't know what the outcome will be."*

As the cauldron of stew, I'm alive with creative possibility.

No wonder we need to look to artists for help. They're the only ones who can show us how to work with something that's vast, mysterious, alive, and messy.

A WAY OF KNOWING THAT HONORS BEAUTY

Of all the significant moments I've had while teaching, one encounter is etched in my memory. After class, a graduate student came up to me. Through heavy tears, she told me she'd always felt she wasn't smart. At the time, I didn't know what to tell her. I reassured her that there was nothing wrong with her intellect. In fact, I highly admired this particular student for her kindness, beauty, grace, and curiosity. Her pain touched me.

Our cultural notion of smart often has to do with one's proficiency with language. When we can confidently put forth a clear, logical argument about something, we're much more likely to be viewed as smart. But as we saw with David Lynch, we can't always say all that we know.

Despite the high value our culture places on cognitive understanding, we were creatures on this planet who learned long before we had formal language. The earliest humans drew on artistic ways of knowing to connect with the natural terrain around them. They looked to flowing rivers, fierce thunder and lightning, the magnificence of a sunrise or sunset, and the curiosities of plant and animal life for guidance and inspiration.

So too, babies don't have well-developed verbal skills. Before expressing themselves through language, babies make meaning from their environments. They experience and learn from shape, dimension, size, and texture.

And so begins our long journey as learners.

Etched deeply into our genes is a profound, sentient way of knowing that doesn't have anything to do with linear thinking and verbal acuity. My student who thought she wasn't smart may be more adept with this other way of knowing—a way of knowing that honors the rich beauty of our animate world.

KEYS TO DEEP KNOWING

The creative process puts us in touch with transcendent energies.

Transformative change doesn't come from solitary struggle; it comes from partnering with the powers that lie under the surface. *That* is when we're brilliant.

At the moment our linear minds give up, we enter a new place where another kind of wisdom lives.

When we admit that we don't know everything, we must *feel* our way to understanding.

Through our capacity for metaphor, we can open spaces that in a logical world *do not exist.*

A metaphor gives you an experience. *It takes you somewhere.*

Our right hemisphere responds sensually to the world. It wants intimacy, feeling, connection, and relationship. That's how it learns.

AWAKENING DEEP KNOWING #3

ONE SIMPLE BRUSH STROKE

I once sat on the bank of the Big Sur coastline at Esalen Institute with a pad of paper, brush, and black ink. Gazing at my surroundings, the thing that most struck me was a cypress tree perched on the edge of the cliff. With one stroke, I drew its branch reaching out over the ocean.

One simple brush stroke was enough to capture its source vibration: REACHING.

Spend some time noticing the organic form of trees, a river, or a cluster of daisies, and then see if you can capture that message in only one or two simple brush strokes.

Just notice *one simple quality.*

Like for example, OPENNESS. Or STRENGTH, or FLOW, or EXPANSIVE.

You might notice the canopy of a tree and it says to you: *"I'm full and lush. I'm in my fullness."* Write in your journal: "What does *fullness* mean for me right now? What guidance does it offer?"

You noticed it for a reason.

Above all, keep it simple. When we make something complicated, we lose its essence.

AWAKENING DEEP KNOWING #4

THE METAPHORICAL WISDOM OF SPORTS, MARTIAL ARTS, AND CREATIVE ARTS

What's your favorite art, sport, or playful diversion? Have you had moments where you felt *at one* with it? Times when you slowed down and connected with a deeper wisdom? What was the special quality of that moment? What guidance does that quality have for you?

Here are some examples.

Gail loves to swim, and swimming often shows up in our sessions. Water is a source of deep support for Gail. Sometimes she's resting in it; sometimes she's moving through it. When challenging things happen in her life, Gail remembers that she's a competent swimmer. She knows how to move gracefully, with a minimum of effort.

Ellen is embroiled in a fierce legal dispute with her business partner. She's stressed out, grieving, and afraid of her partner's motives. But the metaphoric wisdom of her tai chi practice has given Ellen a way to move through this challenging situation gracefully. Her body innately knows how to be strong, centered, and fluid.

And finally, an artist named Sara shared how the practice of calligraphy has changed her life:

> Just the literal practice of it—writing lightly enough for the parts that need to be thin. The variation of pressure is really important and it's been difficult for me because I have a heavy hand. Learning to write more lightly has changed how I live my life. I am learning to be lighter.

What practice—sport, martial art, creative art—takes you into a place of strength, grace, centeredness, and fluidity?

What practice aligns you with Something greater than yourself?

5

BRINGING THE FIELD INTO FOCUS

We have to learn to think in a new way.

~ ALBERT EINSTEIN

THE INTELLIGENT FIELD MOVES US

After receiving my Ph.D., everything in my external world seemed to be nudging me to "get out there and do great things." Fellow students were receiving grants, fellowships, and prestigious tenure-track positions at major research universities. My advisor Mihaly Csikszentmihalyi was excited about my dissertation research and wanted me to publish it. (And I didn't take that lightly, coming from him). Everywhere I went, I met freshly minted Ph.D.'s who were busy writing journal articles, interviewing, and speaking at important conferences. And if that wasn't enough, the University of Chicago was planning to close the department where I'd received my degree. Administrators, faculty, and students were launching a massive fight to try to keep it open by showing how recent graduates (like me) were doing brilliant things in the world. Gulp.

I wanted to be a success story, but I couldn't muster the energy.

I pushed myself. I took a trip alone, secluding myself away at a quiet retreat center to try to focus and get *serious* about my academic work. I managed to claw out an article that was wretchedly dry and boring. I was *not* having fun.

So instead of launching an illustrious academic career, I ended up moving to the wilderness of northwest Montana to hang out with a bunch of hippy musicians.

No matter how much we try, we can't push forward on paths that don't belong to us. We can't move the intelligent field.

It moves *us*.

SOMETHING DEEPER IS CALLING YOU

Tina just spent a considerable amount of money getting a prestigious master's degree at a top university and she has yet to launch the work she wants to do. She's been beating herself up for not being excited and motivated to go out and start her own business. Tina knows she has talent, brains, and ambition, so what's the f*^&%* delay?

Perhaps it's because the intelligent field has something else in mind.

Despite our culture's extreme focus on achieving and producing, our best work (and our best lives) doesn't respond well to pushing. Try as we might, we can't "make" something happen. The apple tree doesn't try to force its fruit to ripen in the winter or spring. It allows its natural life cycle to unfold.

So too, with humans. Things come to us when we're aligned with our own organic energy patterns.

Clients come to me dissatisfied with some aspect of their life. They're bored with their work, unhappy with their family life, or ready to retire but feel there's something more for them to do. From there, we discover creative movement that neither of us expected and vibrational wisdom we didn't know existed.

Just because you can't see it, doesn't mean it isn't there.

The intelligent field will haunt you until you heed its call. It will harass you until you pay attention. It might even give you some physical ailments.

It's not to be dismissed.

To create anything that we want in our lives—a significant relationship, a business, an exotic adventure, a work of art—we need to be in *harmony* with Spirit. When we're stuck or not moving forward with grace, ease, and joy, it's because we're *out of flow*—pushing in a direction that's out of alignment with a larger creative force. Your rational mind may think you should go one way, but Something else wants to move you in a different way.

Our culture views creativity narcissistically— as something that comes entirely from our own efforts, perseverance, and skill. Something that's about us and our own greatness. If we're not finishing that project, if we can't seem to figure out our next career move, if our relationship with our partner isn't satisfying, we believe we haven't *worked hard enough.* So, we get accountability partners, make detailed schedules, take time management classes, and go to counselors.

What's been missing has been an appreciation for the creative realm itself.

Picasso famously said that with every act of creation comes first an act of destruction. We live *within* a creative process—a creative process that is continually destroying and transforming our human-made things, relationships, communities, and institutions.

The Universe is in a continual act of "making" and *we* are its ingredients.

The intelligent field doesn't exist to serve our narcissistic desires—it has its own *independent* wisdom, intention, life force, and direction. But we aren't entirely at its mercy. Instead of being pushed around or dragged kicking and screaming into the next thing, we can engage with it *before* it springs itself on us.

SHIFTING YOUR FOCUS

Alice was worried about her finances. She worked as a free-lance editor, but the work was drying up and she wanted to find something else quickly. She decided to apply for a Project Management position at a non-profit, which made logical sense—the organization's mission was in her field of expertise and as an editor she was already doing project management work. Rationally, this new position seemed to be an excellent way to transfer her skills into full-time employment. Ninety-five percent of career counselors would tell Alice she was making a wise decision.

But Alice and I did a session and consulted the intelligent field. The image that arrived was of a drawstring bag and Alice was inside of it... desperately trying to open it so she could get out. But the intelligent field revealed that the bag Alice was trying so hard to get out of wasn't *ever* going to open. The bag was shut tight and it was going to stay that way.

But that didn't mean Alice would (metaphorically speak-ing) suffocate and die. Rather, the creative movement was in the *opposite* direction, the place that she would never think of looking: the bag's dark interior. Try as she might, her problem wasn't going to be resolved through logic or effort, because the path that was rich with possibility lay in a place *she couldn't see.*

Most of us respond like Alice to such situations: we immediately spring into fix-it mode, not pausing to consult with deep knowing. But the most abundant paths are often ones we can't see through ordinary ways of looking.

Hal is a budding musician. He plays guitar in a band, but there was always some ephemeral thing he couldn't get to. One rainy Wednesday, while waiting for the rest of the band to arrive, he sat behind his friend's drum set and playfully pounded out some beats. It rocked his world. All of a sudden, he had his instrument.

Hal's affinity for the drum had been there all along, he just couldn't see it. Hal could practice for hours every day on his acoustic guitar and be a ho-hum musician. Or he could open space for something new and unpredictable.

Focusing is a beautiful and necessary human skill. Our mind's ability to focus allows us to make decisions, solve problems, get degrees, perform scientific research, and live fruitful lives. Without the capacity to focus, we couldn't operate in this world.

But our proficiency for focusing also limits the probability that we'll have breakthroughs when we need them. Excessive focus keeps us fixated on a narrow scope of possible actions. We can't see other paths, doors, or opportunities.

Creative breakthroughs require a shift of focus.

LOOKING IN A WAY YOU'VE NEVER LOOKED BEFORE

Once again, let's look to artists for some assistance. In *Drawing on the Right Side of the Brain,* Betty Edwards says that artists notice visual information that the rest of us dismiss as unimportant. She writes:

> What prevents a person from seeing things clearly enough to draw them?... A part of the answer is that, from childhood onward, we have learned to see things in terms of words: we name things, and we know facts about them...The left hemisphere has no patience with detailed perception, and says, in effect, "It's a chair, I tell you. That's enough to know. In fact, don't bother to look at it, because I've got a ready-made symbol for you. Here it is: add a few details if you want, but don't bother me with this *looking* business."

Edwards says that beginning art students typically lavish all their attention on the objects or persons in their drawings and then just sort of "fill in the background." But she claims that the negative space—*the space that lies around a figure*—is *more important* than the figure itself. She writes,

"...if care and attention are lavished on the negative spaces, the forms will take care of themselves."

In other words, *the spaces we don't see are more important* than what we typically focus our attention on.

Does Edward's statement *inspire* you?? It inspires me. The artist is paying attention to something that would benefit the rest of us to pay attention to as well. It suggests that *something else* is available for us to see, something that our rational minds don't have the patience to recognize. Aren't you curious what that might be? Where is the negative space in *your* life?

What don't you see?

Gestalt Psychologists use the terms *figure* and *ground* to distinguish between what therapists notice in a therapeutic situation (figure) and what they don't notice or recognize (ground). This distinction is pertinent in our everyday lives as well: Figure is what we notice and pay attention to, while ground is what we dismiss or don't see. Alice was focused on getting a project management job (figure) that would allow her to draw on her existing skillset (also figure). With that as her focus, she couldn't perceive other possibilities (ground) available to her and other skills that she might want to develop (ground).

In our modern culture, we tend to dismiss intuitive and non-verbal knowing, so before we move on, I'd like to bring the intelligent field into focus. After all, if there's no way for us to recognize its wisdom, there is little point in developing the skills to take us there.

There's an oft-repeated story of the Spanish Conquistadors landing on the shore of South America. As the story goes, the natives couldn't see the Spanish ship anchored out at sea because they had no frame of reference for it. But eventually, the tribe's shaman *was* able to see the ship and once he saw it, others could see it as well.

How *did* the shaman on the shore finally see that Spanish ship? The answer is that he had to look in a way that he'd never looked before. Similarly, I am also describing a way of looking. Just as the Indigenous people of South America might not have had a way to see Spanish ships on the water, our culture hasn't had a way to perceive the intelligent field. In the next section, I share the key to seeing it.

HOW TO SEE THE INTELLIGENT FIELD

In Wolfgang Kohler's 1929 book *Gestalt Psychology*, he presents two simple line drawings—one drawing has round lines, the other has spikey lines. Take a moment to imagine two line drawings. (You might quickly sketch them on a piece of paper). One image has only round lines (like a piece of cotton). The other has only straight lines connected at sharp angles to one another (kind of like a spiky star.) It doesn't matter what the images seem to represent—they have no meaning in the traditional sense. Just get a sense of an image that's rounded and a second image that's spiky.

Then pair the nonsense words *takete* and *maluma* to these two images.

I've presented this example to my students many times, and everyone easily matches the words with their corresponding image. Maluma has a soft, gentle sound, so we instinctively pair it with the image that has smooth, rounded edges. Takete sounds sharp, and without thinking about it, we pair it with the image that has sharp, spiky lines.

How do we immediately know that the word maluma goes with the soft and rounded figure and takete goes with the spikey lines? Because of their shape and contour, of course. These abstract drawings have no obvious content other than their *feel.*

We can feel the difference between them.

While cognitive knowing differs from culture to culture because our concepts about things differ, sensory feeling is universal across all cultures. We humans share a common sensory language that operates *independently* from our reasoning.

A sensory language that is pre-verbal, intuitive, and instinctive. Isn't that remarkable?

The psychologist Rollo May wrote about this sensory language in his book, *My Quest for Beauty:* "Beneath our loquacious chatter, there is a silent language...Our common human language is not...something to do with vocal cords and speech. It is, rather, our sense of proportion, our balance, harmony and other aspects of simple and fundamental form."

Our common human language arrives as a body-based, sensual feeling.

On any particular day, you may feel DOWN or UP, LIGHT or HEAVY. Other days you may feel STURDY, GENTLE or UNFOCUSED. Or, LIGHT, ROOTED or CHAOTIC.

These are all qualities of form.

OUR COMMON HUMAN LANGUAGE IS BEAUTY

Dostoevsky claimed that beauty would save the world. I agree. The intelligent field is the source of creative breakthroughs, but if I had to use one word to describe my experience of it, that single word would be beauty.

Our universal human language is beauty.

Whether you're consciously aware of it or not, metaphoric patterns permeate every aspect of your life. If you feel weighted down or heavy, you will respond to your friends, family, and the world in a heavy way. If you feel light or lit up, you will respond to situations and people much differently. These source vibrations under the surface influence everything you do.

One way to discover your own metaphoric patterns is to notice the images that come up when you speak. When you hear yourself express a metaphor, take a moment to appreciate the sentient feel of it. What is it telling you about where you're at, how you're viewing something, or what you want to do? (Or, what you *don't* want to do.)

You may feel like you're slapping a brick wall, trying to get it to move. Or you may feel like an iron wall is pressing against you, squeezing and suffocating you. You may feel that you're walking on your tiptoes. Or perhaps you yearn to "fly the coop." Or, maybe you're feeling creative fire move through you. These subtle feelings are not to be dismissed. They're gold.

They're doorways to a fiercely alive (and very wise) creative terrain.

KEYS TO DEEP KNOWING

The intelligent field has its own *independent* wisdom, intention, life force, and direction. *It* moves *us*.

Excessive focus keeps us fixated on a narrow scope of possible actions. Creative breakthroughs require a shift of focus.

The spaces we don't see are more important than what we typically focus our attention on.

We humans share a common language that operates *independently* from our reasoning.

Beauty—our appreciation of shape, form, harmony, and balance—awakens deep knowing.

AWAKENING DEEP KNOWING #5

SPACE IS REAL

In this chapter, we learned from Betty Edwards that the spaces we can't see are more important than the figures we *can* see. So with that in mind, let's take a moment to connect and identify with space.

Settle into your body, slow your breathing, let your perception go fuzzy, and begin to sense the spaciousness that surrounds you.

> *This spaciousness is real. It's alive.*
>
> *It's pregnant with creative possibility.*
>
> *Keep your awareness here—on the space around you.*
>
> *Take a minute to linger here in this connected place.*

You are still yourself, but you are also the space.

Do you notice that your energy has shifted? Do you feel calmer, more at peace, more settled?

Do you notice that another part of you is now conscious and connected in a way that wasn't available to you before? Perhaps your sense of being has changed?

The more you attend to the intelligent field, the clearer, calmer, and more connected you will be.

6

BREAKTHROUGHS HAPPEN WHEN WE OPEN SPACES WE DIDN'T KNOW EXISTED

Time and Space are real beings, a male and a female.

Time is a man, Space is a woman.

~ WILLIAM BLAKE

IDENTIFYING WITH SPACE

When I'm feeling overwhelmed or upset by something, I do the following little exercise. On a piece of paper, I draw a tiny black square and then I look at it. The tiny black square is whatever's upsetting me; I can visually see how small it is. But *around* that little black square is *space*. When I shift my focus and identify with the space—rather than the problem—my sense of being changes.

I'm no longer a little punk battling against the big bad world.

Any issue in your life that's daunting or overwhelming—a sudden pink slip, a cancer diagnosis, work that feels beyond your skill set, your affair with a married man, whatever—is that tiny square. You don't need to get lost in it. You are not the stress, overwhelm, or emotion you're experiencing.

You're the space.

And here's the remarkable thing: when you identify with the space—rather than with the problem—you have access to fierce creative power. You're connected to Something larger than yourself.

Most of us view creativity as something we go after or do, like the rest of the items on our To-Do list. But creative breakthroughs don't happen through efforting.

They happen when we open spaces we didn't know existed.

My clients often describe it as: "There's space around me now."

If there's one thing you get from reading this book, I hope that it will be the opening of space you didn't know was available to you. In this chapter, I offer several examples of how my clients have done that.

SOME METAPHORS OPEN CREATIVE SPACE AND OTHERS DON'T

Susan had been a competitive athlete and runner for most of her life. She asked me: "What should I focus on as I run the last lap of my life? On a quarter mile track there are four laps for a mile run and I'm clearly on the fourth and final lap."

Energetically feel into that metaphoric reality: This is your last lap on the track and there is no turning back. There is only one way to go and it has a clear end. How does that feel in your body?

Perhaps a little *small?* Like you don't have a lot of room?

Here's an alternative metaphoric lens: your life is a big creative soup (kind of like the cauldron of stew we experienced in Chapter 4, but this time let's give it more broth.)

How does it feel to be an ingredient in a huge bowl of soup?

Does it feel yummy?

There are all kinds of possibilities in this soup—new combinations of tastes, flavors, spices, people to meet, and connections to make. You don't know what's in this soup, you have no idea what might happen or what new flavors might emerge, but won't it be fun to find out? There isn't a beginning or an end; you're simply in the present moment in a beautiful mix of intriguing, lively possibilities.

For myself with this image, I feel a sense of fun, play, and creative aliveness. I love the *potential* in this soup. I also love that it has a boundary (the bowl itself) because that makes me feel safe amid all this swirling aliveness. With a clear perimeter, I can play in the expansiveness, yet I still have healthy containment. I'm not at risk of seeping out all over the place.

Whether we're consciously aware of it or not, we humans employ metaphoric lenses through which we observe our lives. And because our cultural way of looking is linear, it's not surprising that Susan viewed her life as a one-directional track. We spend our lives measuring things—days, hours, our age, our weight, our accomplishments, income, relationships, how many Instagram followers we have, and so on. Self-help books instruct us to create what we want by setting goals, drafting plans, and delineating the steps to get us there. Numbers help us achieve those goals.

So on the one hand, viewing things in a linear way keeps us focused and moving forward. I can't run a business without scheduling my time. If I want to lose ten pounds, it's helpful to keep track of daily calories and weigh myself. But when we presume that linear is the *only* way, we limit our options.

Especially if what we want is a breakthrough.

Solely viewing our lives in a linear way is stressful because it presumes there's a particular place we have to get to and we must keep pushing to get there. Stopping for a moment to shift gears or take a break isn't part of the program.

There's no time to pause to explore the creative soup.

Being a bowl of soup brought spaciousness to Susan's life and got her off the treadmill. It took her out of a place of trying to figure out what she should do during her last lap, and into a place where she could appreciate the abundance of creative possibilities available to her right now.

It opened up very real and palpable creative space.

New possibilities immediately started showing up, like taking her grandchildren on a weekend getaway. Susan noticed herself relishing her time with them in ways she never would have imagined. She's experiencing fun, joy, creative aliveness, and a depth of love and vitality. She doesn't have this available to her when she focuses on what she needs to achieve.

I'm not saying that all goal setting or accomplishment is bad—some of you are in building stages of work or business and you need to stay focused and finish projects. But this lens is so prevalent in our culture that we miss the other lenses we could be looking through.

When Susan shifted her focus away from what she should accomplish, she opened up space for a breakthrough.

SO WHEN YOU'RE STRESSED OR OVERWHELMED, FOCUS ON THE SPACE

Gail is a single mother of three young children. She lives in her parent's basement to make ends meet, works two part-time jobs, and takes night classes for a nursing degree. Yes, Gail is over-the-top busy and stressed by responsibilities, but a vast realm of powerful energy is under the surface, ready for her to draw upon any time she wants to shift into it.

The image that showed up for Gail was an enormous canyon and the source vibration was STILLNESS. Her experience of this energy was profound. In the midst of everything she had on her plate, Gail could palpably feel it. Deeply grateful, she committed, "I'm going to hold stillness in my life because I *do* have enough time for that. I can stop and be still, even if only for a moment." Later she emailed me, "The stillness is always with me."

The year after I had an ovarian tumor removed, I was waiting for a routine dermatology appointment and a wave of fear suddenly flooded through me. There was no reason to be afraid at that moment, but fear isn't always rational. When I tuned in, the guidance was simply to remember the spaciousness around me. So I closed my eyes and directed my attention to the space.

As we learned in the last chapter, this is similar to how Betty Edwards teaches beginning art students to draw. She wants her students to "lavish care" on the space that lies around a figure. Focusing my attention on the space—rather than the problem—gave me an immediate shift. It was calming.

I was no longer alone in this world.

Renee is a very busy married mother of two young children who also runs a small publishing company. She's a gifted writer and artist and always has a gazillion ideas running through her head about all the projects she would like to do. Although good things are happening for her, having so much going on can be overwhelming. Diving into the intelligent field, she received this message:

> *You already have what you're looking for. Notice the space around you—THAT is your answer. You need to know what it's like to sit with all this busyness and ideas and art projects flowing all around you. You don't have to stay in this place of empty stillness because you can't—you're very involved in doing many things. But you know that it's there. Feel this space and let it feed you.*

When Renee shifted her focus to the expansive space, she felt much less weighed down by her numerous responsibilities. Even amid all that was happening, she could operate from a spacious place, allowing a larger creative flow to unfold through her.

When his marriage fell apart, Bill also lost the company he'd started with his wife. Everything he'd built over the past 15 years was gone. He was traumatized and scared, but instead of slowing down to regroup and reflect on his next steps, he insisted on moving forward. He latched onto the advice of a friend who led him into a precarious new financial venture. When Bill came to see me, he was in a tailspin of fear and alarm.

The image that showed up was a spider web and its source vibrations were SPACIOUS and CLEAR BOUNDARIES. The spider web made a lot of sense to Bill and helped him understand how to claim his turf with his friend. If a counselor or therapist had simply told Bill to give himself some space or set boundaries with his friend, it might have been harder for him to follow through. But the spider web made his need for space tangible. He said, "I'm learning that *I* get to define how big my web is—what's inside of it and what's outside of it. And when things pull on my web, I don't have to react."

Jenny just graduated with her master's degree in psychology. She has a family to help support and is eager to start earning an income right away, but she's feeling lost about where to begin. She had some ideas about wanting to lead workshops and was thinking about signing up for an expensive training program that promised to help her get started.

The image that Jenny brought into our session was a bridge. She was on one side of the bridge and the place where she wanted to be (happily working with clients) was on the other side. When I asked her to feel into the bridge image, she said, "I'm solid and heavy. I feel weighed down with responsibilities."

As I did with John, I suggested to Jenny that she instead imagine herself as a bowl of soup. Identifying with this image, she had an immediate shift of energy and a big aha: "Oh, I get it! I'm ready to serve! I don't need to 'get somewhere else.' I'm already where I need to be." Jenny said,

> *I'm a rich soup and I have everything I need. My ingredients are the things that inspire me—literature, characters from novels, connections with people. I keep this soup tasty by stirring it and mixing the ingredients. My soup is delicious for people to eat.*

The soup image helped Jenny understand that she had everything she needed to work with clients and lead workshops. She had a unique career history, a love of people, and a wealth of life experience. She didn't need more training or preparation, but Jenny couldn't see that until she shifted how she was looking. She had to stop focusing on where she thought she needed to go and turn her attention to the rich soup that's already available to her.

Finally, Barbara is a widow with no children and she worries about who will take care of her in old age. Her anxiety has driven her to start drinking in the evenings. The image that showed up in our session was a labyrinth and its vibration was WHOLENESS. As Barbara shifted into it, her anxiety dissipated.

> *I feel present now. In all my striving and searching, I forget my own wisdom, my own connection to Spirit. I can see that my answers will come from trusting myself and just being open. My mind can't figure this out. I've gone on so many journeys in my life, hiking and traveling in new countries where I was just open to whatever I met. I can see that this is just another kind of journey. I don't want to worry so much that I miss this moment in my life.*

Identifying with the labyrinth brought Barbara back to herself... and *then* she got her answers.

Barbara may still take action toward finding a long-term care solution, but she'll be making those decisions from a spacious place of calm. Not fear.

All of us have likely experienced times when we let overwhelm, anxiety, intense emotions, or drama get the better of us. Daily life can be a huge, swirling whirlwind of unforeseen circumstances. We get exhausted at work and snap at our colleagues, we take care of others but forget about ourselves, we worry about the future or get swept up in some crisis that is better left alone. When we get off track, it's so nice to have a place we can rest back into.

No matter what demands you have on your time or what stressors you're facing, there's a field of creative intelligence available to you. I want you to tap it.

KEYS TO DEEP KNOWING

Creative breakthroughs don't happen through efforting. They happen when we open spaces we didn't know existed.

When we *identify with the space*—rather than with the problem—we connect with Something larger than ourselves and receive an immediate shift.

When you think you need to "get somewhere," you miss what's available.

When we alter how we're looking, we can open the intelligent field.

The intelligent field brings us back to ourselves... and *then* we get our answers.

AWAKENING DEEP KNOWING #6

A QUICK SHIFT OF ENERGY

When you feel worried or overwhelmed, take a quick moment to close your eyes and imagine a vast, very peaceful desert terrain. This desert is expansive and you can't see the edges of it.

Then imagine you *are* this desert terrain. You are VAST.

You know what the VASTNESS knows.

Now as you identify with the VASTNESS, where is your overwhelm, worry, or fatigue? It's disappeared, hasn't it? You can't hold VASTNESS and worry together at the same time.

You are either in one place or the other.

AWAKENING DEEP KNOWING #7

FINDING YOUR IMAGES

Sometimes people feel pressure to come up with the perfect image that's marvelous or meaningful. But Spirit has a sense of humor—you might get a jar of mayonnaise or a cartoon character or a small little rock. Please don't put pressure on this.

Whatever image shows up, it's not *who you are*. It's simply a portal into an intelligent field of energy. Believe it or not, *any* image will take you there.

Here are some ideas:

a. Potent metaphoric images often come from the natural world, so spending time in nature is helpful. If you live in an urban environment, go to a park and see what stands out to you.

b. A city will also bring up endless possibilities...a building, garden, streetlight, taxi.

c. See what images arrive in your night dreams, day-dreams, or conversations.

d. Close your eyes, take a deep breath, and then open your eyes. The very first image you see will be a metaphor.

e. The examples in this book will open channels for metaphoric images to come to you. If an image from one of my stories stands out, please use it.

f. Ask yourself how you're feeling right now and how you would *like* to feel. Feelings bring up metaphoric imagery.

g. Just offhandedly come up with *anything*. The very first image that pops into your head. It might be something you saw on your walk this morning or something you remember from years ago.

And last but not least, here's my favorite way to get a quick image:

h. Ask a friend for whatever image spontaneously pops into his or her head. Don't tell her about your question (we don't want her thinking to get involved!) Asking a friend for an image works for me every time. It's fun and takes the pressure off.

THE POSSIBILITIES ARE ENDLESS

The image can be absolutely anything—a letter, car, signpost, or cat. It could be a simple circle, or a snow-globe, cobweb, cave, butterfly, or pond. It could be square in dimension like a house or a field of wheat. It could be vast and endless like the sky, ocean, or the desert. It could be deeply rooted like a tree or ivy. It could be tall and straight like a pine tree or nebulous like a wisp of smoke. It might have a fuzzy shape like a cloud or a clearly defined shape like a door. Some images are expansive, without a beginning or an end—like a river or a horizon line. Some images offer a *connected* feeling, like an underground root system of mushrooms. Some images have an interesting texture.

Again, this image doesn't need to be personally meaningful. In Chapter 1, I told the story of my head-on collision. Lying in the emergency room in severe trauma and pain, I began to relax and heal when my body experienced the lightness of a cloud. Clouds don't hold any personal meaning for me, yet the shift I experienced changed my life.

Your image can be any size. Ask the image what size it wants to be.

ACCEPT WHATEVER IMAGE ARRIVES. LET IT SURPRISE YOU

We're working with Spirit here and Spirit brings surprise. Let the image *choose you*; let it surprise you. The fewer associations you have with it, the better. When you work with images that don't make rational sense, you have more spaciousness available. You'll be much more able to pick up on its energetic quality because your mind isn't busy figuring out what it *means*.

And if there's an image that won't let you go and you don't like this image, I'd strongly suggest going deeper with it. It's coming from a place that's wiser than you.

THE SIMPLER, THE BETTER

Sometimes clients like to come up with elaborate, complex images with lots of characters and things happening. Detailed images are like candy for the mind, keeping it happy figuring out what everything means. But powerful metaphoric images are not complex or pretentious. The image doesn't want you to figure it out; it wants you to *embody* it.

As Einstein once said, "When the solution is simple, God is answering." Keep it simple.

YOUR IMAGES WILL COME TO YOU

Rest assured that your images *will* come to you. All you need to do is be open and welcome them. If you feel stuck, your logical mind is likely dismissing the images that *are* showing up as not good enough or too silly. In Shamanism, we welcome and work with anything that comes.

NOTE: When you have your image, spend some time with Awakening Deep Knowing Exercises #8 and #9 to go deeper into its wisdom.

7

SHIFTING INTO THE FIELD

When we humans have more than we can bear,
the Gods take pity on us and change us into
something else.

~ FROM AN INTERVIEW WITH NOVELIST STACEY D'EVASMO

After a career spent teaching, I started a private practice working with individual clients. My aim was to open up his or her creative process using various modalities that drew on the power of metaphor—creative writing exercises such as fairy tales, playfully engaging with evocative imagery, following revealing slips of the tongue, and so on. Because metaphor is well suited for uncovering unconscious beliefs and perceptions, I presumed that a deep dive into a person's metaphoric patterns would reveal rich material about how she experienced her world.

My presumption was correct, but I was stunned when something else started happening.

Engaging with images in the way I describe in the following chapters opens up what I can only describe as an Other world of intelligent, dynamic energy. This palpable energetic field is independent of our identities and once we open it, we can never predict what will show up. Sometimes the energies are wild and fiery. Sometimes they're gentle, bringing motherly love, creative flow, or a beautiful, delicate lightness. Sometimes they're strong and masculine; sometimes they're deeply erotic. It's not uncommon for indigenous tribal energies, ancient lineages, the Divine feminine, Spirit guides, and power animals to show up.

No matter what the field brings, shifting into its energies brings profound spiritual attunement. When we step into the field, my client and I are no longer our "small selves." We are one with Something greater than ourselves.

I soon realized that my work wasn't going to look like traditional therapy, counseling, or coaching. My primary purpose wasn't to help my clients understand some inner conflict or fear. Nor was it to open a space for them to tap into their own creativity, or help them know how to handle a particular situation, or make a decision about something. Yet these things happened during a session.

My chief mission was to take my clients beyond their thinking to a particular vibrational frequency—LIGHTNESS, DEFINITION, SMOOTH, STRENGTH, REST, EROTIC, WHOLENESS, STURDY, FULLNESS, CIRCUITIOUS, CREATIVE FLOW, and so on. This source vibration would shift them into their fullest, most powerful, hooked up, creative selves.

Their place of full aliveness.

This living field of intelligence will always bring the perfect right vibration for an individual client. But we can never know ahead of time what that will be.

Only this realm knows what you need for your whole life to change.

A THIRD SHAMANIC INITIATION

Maybe I should have predicted that my work with clients would involve accessing the vibrational field because several months earlier, I'd had a third shamanic initiation.

I was hired to teach a course at a graduate school and before the course started, the department head asked me if one of their upper-level PhD students could co-teach it with me. I didn't see any reason to say no, so I agreed, not realizing that this would turn out to be a terrible choice.

On the first day of class, it quickly became evident: These students wanted their peer to teach the course and they didn't want *anything* to do with me. This was much more than a clash of personalities. Something else was going on, something much bigger than me. The students' rage was fierce, archetypal, and overwhelming.

In Jungian psychology terms, I was caught in the students' "complex" or unconscious emotional pattern. These students idolized the teaching assistant, she was the *Good Mother*. And I, unfortunately, was the Bad Mother. To get what they wanted, I needed to be annihilated. (Remember my short discussion of polarity in the Preface. When we're caught in a polarity, no creative movement can happen.)

To step back from my story for a moment, I'd like to emphasize that these kinds of fierce projections are very apparent in today's world. The internet provides open ground for all kinds of conspiracy theories and radical views. And when someone holds the opinion that one side is "God" and the other side is "evil," no amount of reasoning will convince them otherwise. Deeply held beliefs don't budge with rationality or logic. They are archetypal and unconscious.

And at the archetypal level, holding onto beliefs is a matter of life or death. Letting go of a belief can destroy our sense of self, so it must be desperately held onto at all costs.

After suffering through a couple of classes, it was clear I couldn't proceed. I couldn't continue to be in the same room with people who wanted to kill me off. But what was I going to do?? Spending time in therapy trying to figure out how this related to my childhood wasn't going to make any difference. There was no time to create some sort of group bonding or sensitivity training, and it wouldn't have worked anyway. I considered quitting, but this was a required class and I was the main instructor. Walking out in the middle of the term would have left the school in a bind.

I consulted with anyone I thought could be helpful and then the Gods stepped in. A wise artist friend of mine offered some advice that seemed promising: *"Try not being yourself."*

"Before you walk into that classroom, shape-shift into a pure energy form. Teach the class from a place of being pure energy, not from a place of being Kim."

Hmmm, I wondered. Would that work? What would it mean *not to be myself*... to instead be a field of pure energy? How would that feel? Could I speak from this place? Could I teach from that place? How do I maintain being pure energy during a three-hour class?

Before the next class session, I spent some time meditating. As best as I could, I imagined that I was not myself. Instead, I was a vast expanse of energy. Toward that end, reading these words from Eckhart Tolle's book *Stillness Speaks* helped immensely:

> "Most people confuse Now with *what happens* in the Now, but that's not what it is. The Now is deeper than what happens in it. It is the space in which it happens."

Tolle's words shifted me into an energetic space that lay beyond my thinking. I was no longer my small self. Instead, I was a place of deep presence.

I'm not going to lie—I was nervous walking into that room. But despite my fear, *being a field of pure energy* *<u>worked</u>*. It was like I was no longer a solid substance, no longer a 'person.' There was no one there for the students to project upon.

Most importantly, the vibrational frequency of wiping me out wasn't present in the room.

Not only could I teach and speak as a field of energy, but I could also smile and enjoy myself. It was fabulous.

Things were going so well that I decided to experiment and become "Kim" again. I stepped out of being the pure energy and said something that I loved about the course material. Instantly, their rage came at me. I was back to being Bad Mother.

When I taught the class as a pure energy field, there was a clear vibrational shift in the room. There's absolutely no way my ordinary self could have pulled that off.

For the first time, I had directly accessed the intelligent field and facilitated a shift in an entire room. And it *worked.*

In Chapter 5, I share about the shaman on the shore who looked in a new way to see the ship out on the ocean. After he saw the ship, his tribe was able to see it as well. This is what I do in my work with clients. I speak what I'm seeing and experiencing, and then my clients can experience it as well. In the process, they open a new channel of knowing.

Clients describe it as a flood, or surge, of energy. They'll say something like, "When you talked, I had an immediate shift. You said CLARITY was powerful and then it flooded in immediately." Or, "When you said, 'STRENGTH,' I *felt* it. I felt that energy *from* you. The second you said it, I immediately felt it in my body." Or, "I hear that energy in you. When you talk, your words enter and move me. I feel them and that possibility becomes true for me. You say something and it's suddenly *real*."

This is the crucial moment when this realm's potency is unmistakable. We're in a new space that didn't exist before. Something greater than both of us is present.

Faced with a room full of scary people, Spirit taught me something I wouldn't have learned in any other way: *our energy field is real and it's fluid.*

We can BE anything we'd like.

METAMORPHOSIS

Ann's job as a hospital administrator is stressful and drains her energy. She spends her weekends recovering and over time she's gradually let go of the activities that used to make her happy and fill her up. "I feel tired and empty," she complained.

The image that showed up was a dancer, with the thrilling source vibration of WILD.

I wasn't trying to *manifest* WILDNESS for Ann. Once we open the field, I can never predict what will show up and neither can my client. The vibration could have been entirely different—it could have been REST, STRENGTH, PLAYFUL, or whatever.

Again, only the field knows what Ann needs for her whole life to change.

In this case, it happened to be WILD.

And the images aren't *literal,* so the dancer image wasn't bringing Ann some sort of direct message she needed to follow, like: *"Spend your evenings and weekends dancing."* There's no way she would have been able to muster the energy to follow any such instruction. The image is a portal to a field of energy. It's not our task to interpret it.

This work also isn't about positive affirmations. Ann isn't repeating the phrase *"I feel wild"* repeatedly, hoping that something in her life will change. The WILD vibration isn't something outside of herself that she's "calling in" or trying to *extract* from the image. WILD is the source vibration that's here *right now* from the intelligent field. By imagining herself as the dancer, Ann could tangibly *experience it.*

Her dancer image provided the portal to WILD.

This work is about shifting into *another state of being.* Without that energetic shift, Ann would continue living her life as she always has: fantasizing and dreaming about having more fun and feeling more vibrant. But not knowing how to get there.

Mary, a commercial artist, felt bogged down and was having trouble completing projects. In our session, the image of wispy smoke showed up and its vibration was LIGHTNESS. As we settled into LIGHTNESS, allowing it to be as big and expressive as it wished, Mary experienced a wave of deep knowing. First, she realized she wanted to be *physically* lighter, both by losing a few pounds and letting go of some of her physical possessions. But she also realized that her work needed to be lighter—she wanted to be less serious, let go of the burdens she'd been carrying around, and have more fun.

When we're lighter, we can move freely, and this was true for Mary. A couple of months later, Mary told me that she'd started a community press with a group of friends and was teaching experimental poetry classes. These were things Mary had never imagined doing, but after our session she found herself moving in new ways and directions. LIGHTNESS gave Mary a way to meander into places and situations that had previously been elusive.

Harry's longtime girlfriend just broke up with him. His way of dealing with pain is to exhaust himself with work and outside demands, and that's exactly what he's been doing. When he showed up for our session, he was strung out and on edge. The image that arrived was of a deep, still pool of water. It was immediately soothing and comforting and Harry began to relax. He said, "As the deep pool, I don't react to whatever stormy weather is happening on the surface."

A therapist or coach could *tell* Harry that he needs to rest, give himself more space, or set better boundaries, but what do most of us do with advice like that? It sort of goes in one ear and out the other, doesn't it?

The intelligent field makes Harry's self-care *tangible* on a level that's not available to him through goal setting or good intentions. The deep pool is more than simply an idea in his head. He can feel its presence—it's a *living field of intelligence* that he can rest into.

GOING BEYOND YOUR THINKING

I wrestled with the fact that I didn't want my clients to come up with their own ideas about what an image meant to them personally. Having spent so many years teaching, I'd always believed my role was to provide a space where people could come up with their own answers. Why shouldn't I allow people to interpret their images? I was also going against the grain of mainstream image-based therapeutic methods—art therapy, Jungian analysis, dreamwork, and so on—which involve personal associations.

But contrary to my previous training, I became agitated when clients, students, or workshop participants automatically began to interpret an image. Their analyses would *keep them in ordinary thinking* and block their deep knowing.

It would keep them stuck inside the spider's web.

Jumping into your head to analyze an image won't get you to the intelligent field, the place where true magic lives.

I want you to go beyond your thoughts.

It happened less frequently, but it was also painful when clients wouldn't allow themselves to experience the potent life energy available to them. Creative energy that would transform their whole life if they would let it.

Martha was in her 60s and hadn't been in a sexual relationship for a decade. She described this part of herself as "dead" and "numb." When we entered the intelligent field, the image of frozen ground in spring showed up. But although the image was of frozen ground, its source vibration was organically, richly EROTIC. Yes, the ground was frosty, but it was *spring*; the chilled earth was *coming alive*. It was HOT—a richly seductive heat that rouses the growth of spring flowers.

Yummy. (I'd certainly want more of that in my life.)

Unfortunately, Martha would not work with this image because she explained, "I *hate* to be cold." Martha's mind was so wrapped up in her ideas and beliefs about frozen ground and not wanting to be cold that she missed out on a chance to shift into EROTIC energy.

And then there's Elaine, who has worked in the banking industry for many years but has long since grown tired of it. What she *really* wants to do is costume design, but she keeps dismissing that idea. It seems frivolous; she's not comfortable launching into something with unknown financial value.

In our session, the image of a bubble arrived. The source vibrations were WHOLENESS, LIGHTNESS, and FREEDOM. The LIGHTNESS and FREEDOM told me she was untethered and free to do anything she wanted to do. And WHOLENESS had several messages. For one thing, it told her she had everything she needed to be a successful costume designer, including the financial resources to support herself. She was, as they say, "good to go." WHOLENESS wanted her to *claim* the deeply creative part of herself. It was time for her to *own* her gift for design.

Her desire to express it was genuine. Not a fantasy.

But Elaine swiftly rejected the bubble: "Bubbles are fragile; they pop easily and fly all over the place." She was so attached to her negative opinion of the bubble that she couldn't embrace its gift. Beautiful energies of WHOLENESS, LIGHTNESS, and FREEDOM had arrived and wanted to transform her life.

Again, I wasn't trying to manifest these energies for Elaine so she would follow her buried dream. As I said before, I never know what will show up and I'm not invested in my client's choices. But in this instance, Elaine was getting a clear answer.

And here's one last example of how our thinking mind can be tricky (and oh so very smart.)

At a recent workshop, Allen got an image of a bicycle gathering dust in the corner of a garage. The image was static and I wasn't feeling any energy from it, so I asked him for a second image. He said, "I see a bird in a cage." "What does the bird feel like?" I asked. "Trapped. It's fluttering its wings, wanting to get out," he responded. We now had not one but *two* images that represented being static and trapped.

But I could feel the source vibrations—this bird was brimming with LIFE and FREEDOM. It was far from dead and lifeless; it wanted to MOVE. I said, "The bird is free and has a lot of life. Let's let the bird be as big as it wants to be. Let it be as free as it wants to be right now." This message was the permission Allen's deeper self needed and tears welled up. "When you said that, the bird immediately went from the cage into the sky. It's a beautiful, clear day. The bird is so happy to be flying."

Allen saw the bird as trapped because that's how he saw himself.

There was no need to analyze further *why* Allen perceived himself as being constrained and unable to move in his life because he'd already experienced the shift—his body had experienced the energies of LIFE and FREEDOM. Living from this vibrational frequency brought Allen all kinds of fresh possibilities, as he later shared, "I have plans to travel and I'm finding myself exploring things that I'd never considered before. I feel alive in a whole new way."

We each hold beliefs about who we are, how we feel, and what we should be doing at any given moment. But to come up with truly innovative solutions, make discoveries, ignite revolutions, and achieve leaps forward in our understanding, we need to see what lies beyond those beliefs.

Otherwise, we stay stuck.

Despite the roles you're expected to execute, the demands and responsibilities you have in your life, or the dynamics of any given situation, you can shape-shift into *completely different energy at any moment.*

And remarkably, that energetic vibration is not make-believe. It's real.

Our ability to metamorphize is a gift from the Gods and we haven't even begun to tap it.

KEYS TO DEEP KNOWING

In a different vibrational frequency, you get different answers.

Only the intelligent field knows what you need for your whole life to change.

Metaphoric images are *portals* to a field of energy that will shift you into *another state of being.*

Despite the roles you're expected to execute, the demands and responsibilities you have, or the dynamics of any given situation, you can shape-shift into a completely different energy at any moment.

Your energy field is fluid; you can BE anything you'd like.

AWAKENING DEEP KNOWING #8

SOURCE VIBRATIONS

Let's say your image is a dandelion.

What quality stands out? When you feel into it, are you most drawn to the dandelion's shape, size, texture, petals, or color? Whether it's open or closed? Are you noticing its stem? Are you noticing that it's rooted in the ground? Are you noticing that it's open to the sun? Are you noticing that the wind is blowing it?

Don't try to force an answer. Just look at the dandelion in a fuzzy way and some quality about it will come into focus. You're not trying or efforting—you're merely noticing a simple attribute that stands out to you. Trust your deep knowing; it won't steer you wrong.

If you were going to describe this quality with a word or two, what would it be? For example, FOCUSED, CLEAR, SOFT, DISJOINTED, TALL, ROOTED, GENTLE, STRONG, BRIGHT, OPEN (or a zillion other possibilities.)

Then close your eyes and feel into this quality. Let it get bigger. Let it flood through and shift every cell in your body. It's a doorway to a living field of intelligence. Rest into this field.

You are no longer merely your physical body. *You are this energetic quality.*

That quality is the distinct way for you to align with Something greater right now. It's your directional pointer.

NOTE: As a follow-up exercise, try the Awakening Deep Knowing Exercise #9 and draw, write, or dance the quality. Focus on the quality that you noticed, rather than on the whole image of a dandelion: *"I am bright yellow. I love to shine."* or *"I am firmly rooted in nurturing soil. I want to remember to feel the love that's under me."* or *"I have a long stem. It's time for me to be taller in this world."*

8

FROM SEEING TO FEELING

Someday, after mastering the winds, the waves, the tides, and gravity, we will harness for God the energies of love. And then, for the second time in the history of the world, humankind will have discovered fire.

~ PIERRE TEILHARD DE CHARDIN

FEELING WHAT IS TRUE.

Many years ago, well before I started working with clients, I met with an internationally renowned therapist who had developed a popular therapeutic modality using imagery. I was struggling with whether to leave a teaching position and a friend recommended this person to me. I loved teaching at this particular school and I didn't feel like quitting, but little things kept happening that seemed to be signaling me to move on. In the guided imagery session, I saw my hand holding on to my classes and students.

Since I loved teaching at this school, the image wasn't shocking to me. The problem was, there was nothing about the image that gave me any insight about whether to *keep* holding on or to leave. The therapist and I discussed it, and by the end of the hour we concluded that it meant I wanted to stay at my job. So, I signed a contract to teach for the upcoming semester. A few weeks later, I was assigned to lead a daylong seminar in a room that had been freshly painted and carpeted with no ventilation. By the end of that day, I was ill with the most acute respiratory infection I've ever had. It was only then that I realized the image of *holding on* was telling me it was time to *let go*.

The problem is that we can interpret any image in an infinite number of ways. Twenty different people would give me twenty different explanations of my "holding on" image. A Buddhist might see the hand holding on and say that one should always be unattached. An activist might see the gripping hand as strength and say that it means, "go for it." An immigrant might associate it with holding onto family and country. And so on.

Looking back, if I had taken a pause from trying to figure out the meaning of the image and simply dropped into a place where I could feel its source vibration, I would have known what to do. Should I *continue* gripping? Or should I let go?

I would have *felt* what was true.

In previous chapters, we learned that the intelligent field operates independently from what we think and believe. But if that's true, how do we tap into it?

We have to shift from seeing to feeling.

It's a shift from looking at something *with your mind* to imaginatively *feeling* it. Just like you experienced with the two abstract line drawings in Chapter 5.

But how can you know what you're feeling?

THE LANGUAGE OF FORM

When I lived near Glacier Park in Montana, the size of the sky always struck me. It was so *big*. I'm sure the sky isn't more immense in Montana than in other places, but the mountainous terrain gave me a way to see it in a fresh way. With the help of the Rocky Mountains, Montana's sky looks enormous. That is exactly what metaphoric images do for the source vibrations of the intelligent field.

They give us a form so we can see and feel them.

Metaphoric images allow us to see what is hidden below the surface.

The ancient language of form— shape, movement, texture, size, weight, line, and dimension—is embedded deep within our brains and speaks to us in ways that words cannot. It is the source of deep knowing: "That job is too heavy." "I'm ready to grow." "I feel more open now." "I want to settle down."

As I mentioned in the last chapter, I don't care about the role an image plays in everyday life. It doesn't matter whether the image is a ditch or a goblin or a machete or an ugly weed because I'm not working with your traditional understanding of it. (We're not saying, "I see a house and that means I need to settle down." or "I see a weed and that means I'm ugly and unwanted." or "I see a truck on a highway, and that means I need to go on a trip." or "I see a bubble and that means I'm fragile." or "I see a knife and that means someone is coming after me.")

Instead, I'm working with its *form*. That form may not have anything to do with how you personally relate to a particular image, but it has everything to do with how you feel your way into the intelligent field. You are working with the same channel of knowing that looks at a gorgeous flower or piece of cut fruit and finds it erotic because of its evocative shape or texture. Or on the other hand, financial institutions are built with straight, strong, and sturdy lines to give the feeling of safety and stability. EROTIC, STRAIGHT, STRONG, and STURDY are all source vibrations of the intelligent field.

In Chapter 4, I tell the story of painting a vine of flowers down the side of a mask and as I painted, Something greater than myself moved my hand. At that moment, I ceased being Kim as an individual persona. I was in an expanded state of consciousness, *moving as one with Spirit.*

The sensual feeling of the vine is what took me into this expanded state. As I drew the vine's shape and curve, I found myself internally embodying these graceful lines. As I defined them with my paintbrush, I shifted into another realm where I was no longer my small self. I was one with the Divine.

Spirit and I were moving the paintbrush together.

I wasn't *thinking,* "What does a vine look like?" "How should I draw it?" I was merely in the present moment, feeling into its beauty. *When I immersed myself in its form, I entered a transcendent place.*

In Chapter 1, I shared about Zen master Suzuki who, in a moment of extraordinary perception, said, "I had not ceased being myself, but I was also the trees." This is what I experienced. I had not ceased being myself, but I was also the vine.

One way to think of form is that it's the *essence* of a thing—what something is underneath its exterior. As we learned in Chapter 5, our modern way of looking is to focus on the surface or foreground. Our linear minds are busy and active; they're not interested in slowing down enough to engage in something sensual and intimate.

But to enter the intelligent field, we must develop a way of knowing that is comfortable with the language of form.

Just to review, I'm not imagining that I'm *like* this form. Rather, *I am the form*. I'm *identifying with* (becoming) its shape, dimension, size, weight, texture, or movement. That form could be a square, circle, line, flow, a wall, ground, or a triangle. It could be something that's tangled, or bright, or hard, light, or something entirely unique.

"Becoming the form" is what I was doing—albeit unwittingly—when I drew the vine on the mask. It's also what I did in the last chapter when I became the field of pure energy before stepping into a room of people who wanted to kill me.

The same source vibration can come through in a variety of different images. For example, one of my clients is working with sexual energy (or should we say, sexual energy is working *her*.) Her first image was a luscious red rose petal; in a second session, it was soil; in another session, it was a dance. All were portals to the same vibrations of LUSCIOUS, SENSUOUS, and SEXUAL. If I had focused on the meaning of the images, we would have missed the luscious energy. We would have missed the door to the intelligent field.

When we open another channel of intelligence and *become the form*—whether that's a *curvy* vase, an *expansive* field, a *spiral* shell, or whatever—the veil between human and Spirit is blurred and we enter a third space.

We're *one* with the Divine.

A QUALITY OF FORM WILL TAKE YOU INTO THE FIELD

At any given time, each of us needs different things: some of us need better boundaries, some of us need rest, some of us need to let our wilder side out, some of us need to soften, some of us need clarity and discipline, some of us need strength, and so on. You get the particular shift that you need because different shapes, dimensions, textures, and movements transport you into different vibrational states.

Metaphor is a language of connection and relationship—*your* relationship to this image. You might get an image of a house and what you notice isn't that it's square or sturdy. What you notice is its pink color. Or that its roof has an interesting texture. Or how very tiny it is. You're connecting in a sensual way with this image and noticing what you notice.

Let's say your image is a pillar. We think of pillars as having good form since they're used to support buildings. But perhaps when you look at this pillar, you notice that it looks disjointed, confusing, or like quicksand.

In other words, *despite what you think its qualities should be, what do you notice*? This image is in relationship to you. The primary quality that you notice (whether it makes sense or not) is the source vibration that's working you right now. It's your portal to the intelligent field.

GOING DEEPER INTO SOURCE VIBRATIONS

Kathy is going through a daunting divorce. Her husband always called the shots in their marriage and she's afraid of being bullied. The image that showed up in our session was a yellow gladiolus flower. While it was pretty and flexible (it could bend with the wind), what was apparent to Kathy was that this gladiolus flower could *hold its form.* Even in stormy weather, the gladiolus blossom would keep its shape. This was important deep knowing for Kathy.

Having a *way* to hold her form made a huge difference when Kathy met with her husband and their attorneys. "It worked!" she exclaimed. "Being the gladiolus kept me out of my head and my fears. I could feel the energetic shift in who I was being. I held my form!"

As the gladiolus flower, Kathy *IS* good form.

Amy recently moved back to the US after living abroad, married to a wealthy international banker. She is newly divorced and eager to establish herself in a career. She wants to start earning money, but she's been stuck. Despite her strong desire to get back into the workforce, she can't get herself to move forward with this plan. What showed up during the session was a muddy pond.

The *texture* of the pond is what was present for Amy—it was MUCKY. As Amy identified with the muckiness and allowed its energy to move through her, something deep broke loose. She was accustomed to the hard-driving world of business and expected it to be her career path, but the MUCKY energy was precisely the opposite. It was slow, warm, and nurturing. For the first time in years, Amy let down her walls and allowed herself to sink into Something else.

She tearfully confided that she'd always had a secret dream of writing a novel.

Do you see how identifying with the dark mystery of the mucky pond took Amy into an entirely *different* place of wisdom? The mucky pond offered her a *shift of BEING* away from the rigid, aristocratic way of life she was familiar with and into the dark mystery of the unknown. An image with clearly defined lines (like a desk, a pen, or a writing pad) wouldn't have gotten her in touch with her true desire. Neither would something that was strong, fiery, or light, for that matter.

Amy needed to shift into her own rich, messy, warm creative terrain. MUCK is what allowed that to happen.

The source vibrations of the intelligent field will align you with your true path. It's about who you *really* are under the surface—under your acquired mannerisms, personality traits, social roles, histories, and conditioning. And yes, even under your prestigious degrees and credentials.

Dana has fiery creative energy. She's a natural performer and when she unleashes her creative fire, it wakes up the part of you that's been asleep. Her artistry is oversized and out of the box; it's not restrained, polite, or pretty.

Dana struggles with the fiery part of her nature and tends to hold it back. "I want to be the good girl; I don't want to hurt anyone," she tells me. "I want to be agreeable. I want to fit in." She's afraid that if she unleashed her full fire, it would be way too disruptive.

And it's true—her fiery energy isn't at all concerned with being pleasant, good-natured, or fitting into the norm. Its mission is to be as big, wild, and fiery as it can be. It's not here to uphold traditions; it's here to break them.

But in our session, the image that showed up wasn't fire; it was a volcano. The volcano is massive yet defined (it has a clear perimeter), and its energetic quality is SOLID and STURDY. As the volcano, Dana is incredibly grounded and strong—after all, she's *embedded* in the earth. She's not the fiery energy; she's the *sturdy mountain* from which intense flames can erupt.

Do you see how a volcano would vibrate energies of STRENGTH and STABILITY? I can't think of too many things sturdier than a mountain.

As the volcano, Dana will not get lost in the fire, nor will she hurt anyone. Dana can handle the fire; it's not going to throw her off her game. In whatever situation she's in—with family, colleagues, friends, and community—her mountain exudes calm and sturdiness. She has an intrinsic ability to keep her form.

PLAYING WITH SOME EXAMPLES

Let's say an image of a cave has come to you. Most of us might close our eyes and visualize ourselves *inside* of the cave, or perhaps next to the cave, or on top of it. But again, to open the intelligent field you need to *be* the cave.

Actors don't analyze their characters from a distance; they *are* the character. Having a tangible experience of *being* Annie Oakley of the Wild West is much different than merely having an intellectual understanding of her. Remarkably, we don't have to be trained actors to be Annie Oakley. That's something a 5-year-old can do.

If I told you, "Be a tiger," I'm sure you wouldn't have much trouble prowling, roaring, and behaving like a wild animal. Your imagination and sentient body would know what to do. You wouldn't be "part of" the tiger. You wouldn't be *inside* the tiger or *on* the tiger.

You would *be* a tiger.

Isn't it astonishing that our human capacities allow us to do that?

Now go back to the image of a cave, which is trickier.

First, close your eyes and imagine that you're *inside* a cave. What do you notice? What are you feeling?

I'll share what I'm experiencing. First, I'm feeling cold. I also don't like being in this dark place all by myself. I'm feeling confused—I'm not sure what I'm supposed to do here.

Now, imagine that you're not *in* the cave, *you are the cave.* *Being* the cave will feel very different.

What do you notice about the cave's form? Start with its perimeter so that we get a sense of where its edges are. What is its shape? How big is it? To be the cave, our energy field needs to be this *entire* shape and size, not just part of it.

Take a moment to close your eyes and make this bodily shift into being the cave. (It's not necessary to close your eyes, but it helps reduce distractions.)

How does it feel to be a cave? What impressions are coming to you? What does the cave *want?* How does it want to move? What quality of the cave stands out for you? How is this quality relevant in your day-to-day life, circumstances, and relationships? It's come to you now for a reason. How is its guidance helpful?

You can't do this wrong—all you're doing is opening up another, non-cognitive, way of knowing. Simply welcome any thoughts or insights that come.

Here's what happened for me. First, I'm sensing a cave with a round, circular shape, so I imagine myself and my energy field as a large, solid, round stone structure. It's big, much bigger than my physical body.

As a cave, I notice my *WHOLENESS*—I have everything I need. I'm not looking for or needing anything else to complete me. I'm very happy to simply be myself, with all my own wisdom and creative resources. I also feel STURDY and I love that feeling. It gives me the deep knowing that I can take care of myself. That's a helpful thing for me to know right now, as I've gone through some changes financially and I've been worried about the cost of long-term care for an elderly family member. But as I rest into WHOLENESS and STURDINESS, these fears aren't present. Spirit is telling me: *"You got this. You're gonna be fine. Don't worry."*

What message does the cave have for you?

What might the cave be telling you about what you want, or how you want to be? This cave is bringing you a shift in *who you're being*. That's a considerable gift.

Although your responses might be different from mine, I'm going to presume that *being inside* the cave and *being the cave* were very separate experiences for you.

Once again, you're not *inside* the image. You're not *next to* the image. You *are* the image. If you're working with a house, you're not an object *inside* the house—like a door or a table or even a room. *You're the house itself.* Imagining yourself inside the house keeps you in ordinary thinking. Imagining yourself *being* the house takes you into the magic of third space.

If your image is the ocean, you're not floating on top of it, or swimming, or (god forbid) drowning. You *are* the ocean.

As I sit with the ocean image, what comes to me is EXPANSIVE, POWERFUL, and UNHARNESSED. Those are great energies to tap into.

Being the image isn't something that can happen in ordinary reality, but you're not looking in an ordinary way. You're looking with the part of you that understands and recognizes beauty. The part that knows you're not separate from the rest of the cosmos, that you're connected to other living things through an energetic field. You are looking with the part of you that is deep and sentient, the part of you that can feel subtle energy. The part of you that is connected to Something greater than yourself.

This is deep knowing.

Let's be a box for a moment. A box can bring super helpful energy, but it can also be tricky because our culture has a negative view of boxes. (People automatically think a box means they're "closed in." But again, we're *not inside* the box, we *are* the box. Being inside the box is ordinary knowing. 'Being the box' brings us into a third space.)

Take a couple of conscious breaths, close your eyes, and move your awareness down into your body and then out into your energy field. Then feel into the perimeter—the square shape—of a box that's larger than your physical body and *become* it.

What do you notice?

Here's what I sense: I am solid and secure. I have a very sturdy bottom—people can push on me, and I will not tip over. I have a lid that I can close or open at my choosing. My corners and edges are clear and defined and this clarity and definition increases my feeling of strength. To be honest, I'm noticing how much I love being a box.

In fact, I didn't think of this before I suggested being a box, but these energetic qualities of STRENGTH, CLARITY, DEFINITION, and STURDY are useful to me right now in this very moment. Because as I write this paragraph, I'm waiting for the local judge to call me about an illegal right turn I made at a red light. (Oops.) It's a phone trial and I'm feeling scared because I don't want the ticket to go on my driving record. But now, taking a brief moment to connect with the field, I feel wise, intelligent energy showing up to support me.

In case this all seems too challenging and abstract, I'd like to remind you that the energies of the intelligent field are constantly informing and guiding you. It's the innate wisdom that kicks in when you walk into a room that feels heavy. Or make a decision that brightens you up. Or when you sit by a pool of water and immediately feel calmer.

When you want to experience expansive possibility, perhaps you go to the desert or climb a mountain so you can look out over a vast valley. When you need to relax, you may go to a peaceful lake. When you want to let go of the past, perhaps you get on a canoe and glide down a river. When you yearn for depth, you visit an old-growth forest or a sacred site of ancient stones. When you want to feel stimulated, you visit a busy city. These places—sea, river, mountain, desert, city—have unique sensory forms that evoke distinctive source vibrations.

Isn't it time you got to know this part of you?

Maybe this all seems excessively simple. Perhaps you're thinking, "So what? My image is a table and it feels STURDY. Who cares? How does that help me figure out what to do with this job I hate or how to rebuild my relationship with my daughter?"

Take a moment, close your eyes, and know that this table is no longer sitting in front of you. Now it lies in a third space. You can't see it, but you *can* feel into its form and you sense the square STURDINESS of it. Then step into it and *become* the STURDY table.

Feel the STURDINESS in every cell of your body.

This is an entirely different energetic space. It's a different place of BEING.

Many of us spend our time analyzing and figuring things out from a safe distance. This is not that. This time, *you* have changed.

More than simply improving your relationship with your daughter, you'll find yourself operating from this new STURDY place in *every* area of your life. You'll be STURDY with your colleagues. You'll make decisions with more ease. You'll find yourself being clearer with people, not getting lost in confusion, ambiguity, or fuzzy commitments.

Dynamic creative energies swirl under the surface and they take form so that we can know them. While our minds insist upon clear facts and concise answers, *form, shape, direction, size, weight, texture, and movement* speak to a deep part of us. This ancient language aligns us with the creative powers of the Universe.

By the way, the judge and the presiding police officer just called. I'm clearly guilty, but while they spoke and presented the evidence against me, I imagined myself as the box. When it was my turn to respond, I confirmed that I had made the illegal turn. (Boxes are clear and defined—there is no wigginess or fuzziness about them). Then the judge *dismissed* the ticket.

I'm telling you, this shit works. (But please don't make any illegal right turns.)

KEYS TO DEEP KNOWING

Our modern way of looking is to focus on the surface or foreground. But to enter the intelligent field, we must develop a way of knowing that is comfortable with the language of form.

We have to shift from <u>seeing</u> to <u>feeling</u>.

We're not *thinking* a particular form; we're *feeling* it. We're *immersing* ourselves in it. We're *identifying with* (becoming) its shape, dimension, texture, size, weight, or movement.

You get the particular shift that you need because different shapes, dimensions, textures, and movements transport you into different vibrational states.

When we '*become the form,*' the veil between human and Spirit is blurred and we enter a third space. We're *one* with Something greater than ourselves.

The ancient language of form is embedded deep within our brains and speaks to us in ways that words cannot. It is the source of deep knowing.

The source vibrations of the intelligent field align you with your true path. It's about who you *really* are under the surface—under your acquired mannerisms, personality traits, social roles, histories, and conditioning.

AWAKENING DEEP KNOWING #9

WRITE, DRAW, OR DANCE THE ENERGY.

I love this exercise and do it nearly every day. Call to mind the image you're working with and feel into its primary qualities. Then write, draw, or dance the energy of the image.

Whether writing, drawing, or dancing, when we work with statements that aren't literally true—such as *"I am the sofa"*–it takes us to a third space.

Here are some examples:

> *"I am the forest and I have a perimeter. I am not out all over the place. I am strong and solid. I know who I am. I'm full of peace* <u>*because*</u> *of my boundaries. My boundaries give me peace."*

> *"I am the loose pile of pink satin ribbon. I'm resting right now, but I don't want to rest. I want to move. Will*

you let me move, please? Let me move so I can unwind. It will feel so good to unwind. I want to unwind."

"I am the dark, pulsing depth. Thank you for dropping into me. I'm always here, but people don't take time out to notice me. This is where it all is, the beginning of it all."

No matter where I am or what I'm doing, this exercise shifts my energy, offers insight and guidance, and takes me into deep knowing.

AWAKENING DEEP KNOWING #10

YOU CAN AWAKEN DEEP KNOWING AT ANY TIME OR PLACE.

Take a pause and tune into your environment. Where are you? What's around you? What do you notice?

Choose one thing that you notice and sensually tune into it—let your body feel into it. You might also do the Awakening Deep Knowing #9 exercise as well.

Here's an example of mine:

The other night I went for a swim in a lake. I was alone, the sun had just set, and the water was cold and filled with algae. Fog partially hid the tall pine trees surrounding it.

I've just listed several images and qualities: mucky (algae), cold, dark, being alone, foggy, tall (trees), and perimeter. Each of those qualities would have taken me into a very different energetic place, but what stood out for me on this particular evening was the shape of the lake—it felt like a womb.

So *womb* is the portal I stepped into. The message arrived: *"I am the womb. I am whole and complete and I'm ready to birth something."*

I *am* ready to birth something; *I can feel it.*

CULTIVATING DEEP KNOWING

Rest. Rest without the need to become. Rest in Being.

~ KATHLEEN DOWLING SINGH

Many of us believe that we must go to a guru, spiritual master, priest, or rabbi for an experience of the Divine. Or to receive spiritual guidance we must pray or interpret messages from our dreams. In both cases, we are separate from Spirit—either by another person, or by our own intellect.

I would argue that most of us want *an intimate, lived connection with higher wisdom.*

An attunement with Something greater than ourselves.

Guided visualization and other image-based therapeutic modalities have become increasingly popular in recent years, and with good reason. But merely working with images won't bring you into third space and intimacy with the Divine. To do that, we must shift into the relational and aesthetic way of knowing that's associated with the right cerebral hemisphere.

I call it *deep knowing.*

I hesitated to bring my shamanic initiations into this book; I'm sensitive to cultural appropriation. I haven't been trained by indigenous shamans and I don't work with the intelligent field in the same way. But the truth is, shamanic power is not limited to geography or culture. In the end, I couldn't complete this book until I recognized and owned my own shamanic experiences.

Shamanism is direct experience of the sacred. That's what this book is about.

To help you have that direct experience, here are seven things to keep in mind.

DEEP KNOWING IS A CHOICE

Just as in Shamanism, deep knowing is not passive—it requires something from you.

We're not passively analyzing an image's symbolism or what it means in a particular culture or context. We are aligning with *real energy* and allowing that energy to *express through us.*

You make a choice whether you want to step into that or not.

In the last chapter, we met Dana. Forgive me for repeating this one last time (it's so challenging to unhook from our conventional way of looking and easy to slip back into it.) Dana isn't thinking she is *like* the volcano. She's not visualizing the volcano, she's not meditating on the volcano, she's not sitting with the volcano, and she's not trying to extract energy from it.

She IS the volcano.

There's a profound difference.

And for Dana to *be* the volcano, *she must be willing to shift her energy*. Remember, metaphor has the *power to take her somewhere,* but she must allow the shift.

If you get the image of a river and the source vibration is FLOW, you have a choice whether you want to sit on the bank and watch the water flow or... BE the FLOW. If you get the image of a skyscraper and the source vibration is STRONG, you could say, "Yeah, that's great. I really do need to be stronger" and then go on about your life as normal. Or you can be STRENGTH.

It's your choice.

DEEP KNOWING IS A PARTNERSHIP

Once again, recall the story I told in Chapter 4 of drawing the vine on the mask. As I drew, I became the vine and became one with Divine energy. The persona of Kim was gone.

Many years later, that experience still informs my understanding of deep knowing. In that moment of becoming one with the Divine, *I met Spirit as an equal. We painted the vine together.* That experience wasn't just bestowed upon me. I had to meet it.

I had to show up and say yes to the partnership.

Artists often say that they experience the presence of Divine energies when they create their art. Whether through writing, dance, painting, whatever—they're in a sensual partnership with Something greater than themselves.

But this partnership isn't limited to the province of artists.

The metaphoric image that takes you into sacred partnership could be a pumpkin, or a pool of water, or a snake. Whatever that image is, it's a lifeline back to your true self. When you lose your form, get off track, become frazzled, sink into self-pity, or unload on your husband, the image can take you back to third space.

When you partner with Spirit, you're in third space—a vibrational place where Divine intelligence can move through you. A place where you can flourish.

DEEP KNOWING IS SIMPLE BUT NOT ALWAYS EASY

Aligning with your own deep knowing is not necessarily easy. We all have fears, addictions, unhelpful relationships, parental voices, and ingrained ways of thinking that cause us to lose connection with ourselves. We all have certain things that pull us out of our own sacred alignment.

In my work with clients, what shows up is the deepest shift that needs to happen. This work isn't light or easy. It's not about skimming the surface of spirituality. We can't align with Spirit if we're in our addictions, fear and phobias, ego, negative patterns, or whatever.

As a consequence, the desired shift will likely be the opposite of how you typically operate. People who are too busy will get the source vibration of REST. People who make things heavy will get the vibration LIGHT. People who are resistant to spending time with themselves will get the message to let go of external commitments and go inward. People who feel trapped will be invited to move into FREEDOM. People who habitually feel responsible for everyone will get the message to be SMALL. People who have a problem with boundaries will shift into CLARITY and STRENGTH. And so forth.

There's a *shift of being* that wants to be made, and that shift will be your core challenge. (After all, if you didn't have more growing to do, you would be a saint.)

It's hard to let go of what we know, even when it's clearly not good for us. We stay in lousy relationships, drink too much wine at dinner, engage in co-dependent relationships, whatever. Our behavior patterns are ingrained and comfortable. We learned them early in life and undoing them is difficult. It's challenging to trust another way.

In Chapter 7, we met Harry. He's going through a stressful situation and his way of dealing with stress is to push himself even harder. In the session, a deep, still pool of water showed up and Harry was finally able to shift into a relaxed state. The pool of water made Harry's self-care *tangible.* Even though relaxing isn't something that Harry is comfortable doing, an entire field of intelligence showed up to help him make the shift. In this case, into DEEP and STILL.

When we viscerally experience the intelligent field, it's easier to shift into it.

DEEP KNOWING FEELS RIGHT

Take a moment to recall a time when you finally made a clear decision about something you'd been struggling with, and you knew it was the right choice. After you made that decision, something inside you probably felt settled in a way that it wasn't before. It's like your nervous system—that had been on high alert—could now relax.

That's what we're going for here. Deep knowing happens when we *energetically feel* what is true. There's an energetic place that your body *wants* to shift into—an energetic vibration that will feel good, expansive, and right. Even if the message is to grieve, or become smaller, or rest, it will feel like a peaceful deep "ah" as you finally allow yourself to settle into what's true.

An image will help you find that space.

Many of us think that someday Spirit will give us a map or speak to us in a clear voice with specific directions. But divine wisdom is neither verbal nor cognitive; it comes to us intuitively, through form and feeling.

Deep knowing will strengthen your sense of self in this world. Even though your thinking mind might tell you you're a failure or everything is hopeless, another part of you will know something else.

DEEP KNOWING IS SUBVERSIVE

In the last chapter we met Amy, who had a buried desire to write a novel. Amy's family and friends viewed creativity as superfluous and writing a novel was far from anything she envisioned doing. Her social life involved hanging out with business executives and she liked that lifestyle. When Amy aligned with the MUCK, she did so at the expense of her own internal (and external) judgments about the value of creative work.

In other words, the intelligent field's wisdom is entirely *independent* of social norms, personal desires, your training, or cultural conditioning. It doesn't care whether you follow the dictums of polite society. It doesn't care whether you're afraid or whether your mother will have an issue with it.

Joan of Arc comes to mind. Once her inner vision took hold of her, she no longer listened to anyone else. Her family, friends, and church no longer had authority over her life.

The philosopher Henry Corbin wrote, "The mystic's visionary capacity frees him from collective norms." When you begin to trust your own visionary power over your communities' voices, norms, and rules, you've stepped into subversive territory. You're not longer bound by the authority of the collective.

An *inner* authority has claimed you.

DEEP KNOWING IS ANOTHER WAY OF BEING

We also met Kathy in the last chapter. Kathy is going through a challenging divorce and her image was a gladiolus flower. The gladiolus wasn't an "idea" in Kathy's head. It's an alignment of her *being* with a creative intelligence that's much larger than her. The gladiolus gives Kathy a third space: a place to let Something greater flow through her.

As the gladiolus, Kathy *IS* good form.

Several years ago, I injured my back. My spine is fused with two metal rods from the car accident I mentioned in Chapter 1 and a disc below the fusion went out of position. I was in terrible pain and my physician told me it would take many months to heal.

When I tuned in, I saw an image of a horizon line—the place where the sky meets the land.

Of course, I had no idea what this image meant. Instead, I've spent the past years feeling into its guidance and direction. The horizon line is very RESTFUL (horizontal lines have a restful feel), yet very, very FOCUSED—the horizon line EXPANDS infinitely in two very precise ways—to the left and the right. The source vibrations of REST, EXPANSIVE, and FOCUSED bring an awareness of something I can't name, but I experience energetically when I shift into it.

This simple horizontal line has shown me how to live my life at a deeper level, with more clarity, definition, and integrity. It has shown me how to focus on things that are essential and let go of things that aren't. It's helped me live more fully in my own skin, firmly planted in my own life. It's shown me how to trust, ease up on my need to control, and let the universal creative flow work through me. The horizon line is my third space—my place of sacred alignment.

This incredibly simple image has brought my attention to what's truly important. It's also given me a place to rest into and heal.

The horizon line isn't a tool. It's a *space* I'm growing into.

DEEP KNOWING IS RESTFUL AND UNHURRIED

Native American youth go on vision quests to get images that will guide them for their entire lives. They spend a lifetime attempting growing into one potent image. Unfortunately, that's not how our culture operates.

Our intellects are lightning quick. They want instant answers and *they want them now*, gosh darn it. I know, I know—we're all busy. I get frustrated too. I can't even stand to wait in line at the grocery store for five minutes.

While the intelligent field *does* provide an instant shift of perspective, fully expanding into your highest self is a process. If I had immediately understood the horizon line, I would have said, *"Great. I get it! What's next? Now I can go jump into the next thing!"* I wouldn't have discovered the deeper, stiller place within me.

There wouldn't have been a sacred alignment for me to find.

Like all humans, I'm not perfect. It's a spiritual practice for me to keep settling into this energetic space. My negative thinking can pull me out of it, along with my addictive patterns, or fear that I'm not working hard enough, or whatever. But when I notice I'm anxious, confused, or overwhelmed, I shift back into the horizon line.

And I come back into right relationship with Spirit.

I have always loved a southern room in my home that has bright coral curtains. When I shut the curtains on a sunny day, the whole room has a pink glow. I'm immersed in a color bath. That's what happens when we're in third space—we're immersed, not only in answers but also in a *way of being* in the world.

As one client remarked, "This didn't just *give* me answers; it *imbued* me with answers."

You have your own sacred place of alignment—a third space that will bring you unimaginable possibilities, as well as a flow, grace, ease, strength, and clarity that you didn't know were so readily available. A place where you're aligned with your true path.

Once you've discovered it, you'll spend the rest of your life settling into it.

When you're in the right energy, things *happen.* You'll cook dinner and spontaneously come up with the perfect right solution for your marketing campaign. You'll effortlessly sit down and write that letter that you've been putting off. You'll say "no" to the extra donut without thinking about it. You'll wake up in the morning with a renewed sense of clarity. You'll stand in your power in situations that used to demean you. You'll find your voice with colleagues. Those things are effortless because you're in a place where Something else can move through you.

You're hooked up.

Source vibrations have been FIERCE when they needed to get my attention, and STRONG and STURDY when I was going through a cancer scare. Working on this book, the energies have been LIGHT, GRACEFUL, and EXPANSIVE.

Many of us ask, "What should I do?" but the more important question is, "How should I *BE*?"

How should I *be* so that I get the answers I need?

How should I *be* so that I have a successful, happy life?

How should I *be* so that I can heal from this illness?

How should I *be* so that I can meet my soul mate?

Our lives unfold from who we are being.

Harry is a pool of water.

Kathy is a gladiolus blossom.

Dana is a volcano.

I am a horizon line.

What are *you*?

Depending upon who we are being at any given moment, we see things differently. We have different answers.

Deep knowing is a shift from *doing* consciousness to *being* consciousness. It's a shift from trying and efforting to letting things *come to you.* It's a shift from anxiety to deep peace, aloneness to connectedness with Something beyond you. You have strength in situations where you used to unravel. You energetically feel at ease, even with more on your plate than you think you can handle.

You're whole and fully alive. You're hooked up.

KEYS TO DEEP KNOWING

To partner with the Divine, we have to shift into an intimate, sensual, relational way of knowing.

Deep knowing is not passive.

The metaphoric image is a lifeline back to your true self. When you lose your form, it can bring you back to third space.

When you begin to trust your own visionary power over your communities' voices, norms, and rules, you've stepped into subversive territory. You're not longer bound by the authority of the collective. An *inner* authority has claimed you.

Our lives unfold from who we are being. Depending upon who we are being at any given moment, we see things differently and have different answers.

AWAKENING DEEP KNOWING #11

PLAYING WITH SIZE

Size shows up frequently when we work with metaphor.

If you've been hiding your gifts, not speaking up when you need to, or you'd like your work to have a larger impact, you can call on the energy vibration of BIG.

And although many of us may feel the need to be bigger, there are also times when it's helpful to be SMALL. Sometimes workshop participants are embarrassed when their image is small and ordinary like a tennis ball. But here's what's true: *it's refreshing to be small in this world.* If you're feeling confused or overwhelmed, worn-out, scared, disconnected from yourself and your inner voice, or you're finding yourself taking on other people's problems, being SMALL will take the pressure off. It will reconnect you with deep knowing and make things manageable again.

Playfully come up with some random image for yourself, become the image, and then let it expand to its proper size. What size feels good to you?

If it's SMALL, you might affirm:

> *"I am whole and little. I can only deal with a certain number of things at any one time. I'm not big enough to take on more than that."*

If it's BIG, you can affirm:

> *"I am big enough to handle anything that comes my way. I let myself be seen. I'm ready to take on more responsibility."*

On any given day, there's a size that's right for you. What size are you today?

A couple of months ago, I was feeling timid, tired, and not up to the task I had in front of me—sending out a promotional email to announce an upcoming class. I tuned in and saw myself as a tiny pink flower.

I energetically shifted into SMALL *and then* I was able to send out the email.

One might think that to send out the marketing email, I should imagine myself as big. That's what all the marketing, self-help, and business books promote, right? But actually, it's often the opposite. I needed to remember how little and inconsequential I was and how little and insignificant this marketing email was. SMALL took all the pressure off and allowed me to do the task with ease.

The artist Maira Kalman said, "Think small is my new motto. It helps me handle the complicated too-muchness of it all." I agree.

Lauren is an exceptionally creative person with a zillion ideas and tons of energy. She's an artist and is creating a business that includes dance performances, video art, writing, teaching workshops, and coaching. In our session, the business told her it wanted to be small:

> *Keep me small for right now. Put your ideas into a small form. Don't get too big. Keep me small, so I can grow into something.*

What size does *your* project want to be?

CONCLUSION

CREATIVE POWER

Something from another world is alive inside [us] now....It alters the nature of our psychological structure. It alters how we see ourselves and how we see the world in which we live.

~ STEPHEN BUHNER, ENSOULING LANGUAGE

It's taken me ten years to write this book.

As I shared earlier, the shamanic initiations took a few years to accept. I also needed time to understand my work better and grow into it. And I spent a few years trying to satisfy those who wanted techniques. I'm glad I spent the extra time to tease out what I'm teaching and how, because it helped me come around to this truth: I don't care about techniques.

I want you to know this realm exists so you'll shift your attention to look in its direction.

We live in a culture that's all about getting, achieving, and pushing ahead. Techniques tend to feed that mindset—a mindset that tells us we don't need to make a fundamental shift. We can just do a quick technique and then get on with our lives as usual. Most of us have little incentive to pause and attune with something deeper.

But deep knowing is not a technique. It's a *way of being.*

The shamanic initiation experiences gave me direct knowing of the intelligent field and that direct knowing is the most important gift my clients receive from me. I want to give that to you.

Knowing this realm is real is what will allow its energies to touch and move you. And that makes sense, doesn't it? Because otherwise, we would just dismiss a potent dream or visionary experience. Although it may have been compelling, it doesn't change our life. Perhaps we feel different for an hour or a day or even a week, but eventually, we forget about it.

Believe me. I was the queen of dismissal.

The notion that we humans are part of Something greater than ourselves is repeated so often it's a cliché. But although few may argue with this idea, our conventional ways of perceiving don't allow us to see or experience this partnership. To our rational thinking, if nothing appears to be there... then it's nothing.

But this is not nothing.

I've never been interested in the occult, crystals, chakras, incense, or even meditation. I do not take drugs and I'm solidly pragmatic. So it never ceases to amaze me that I'm a voice and champion for a non-ordinary realm of intelligent energy.

But I tell you this: intimate connection with Spirit and a direct experience of the sacred is hard-wired into the right hemisphere of our brain.

We have the capacity; we just don't use it.

Your creative capacities are what allow you to engage the intelligent field.

It's become commonplace to acknowledge that we are creative beings, but we humans have the means to create on a level beyond what we can imagine.

Our traditional ways of knowing don't make use of the vast intelligence at our disposal. They don't offer us a way to intimately connect with a lively, intelligent, deeply wise world. Traditional ways of knowing view the world as smaller than us. We're led to believe we just need to do a better job of controlling things.

But in the shamanic worldview, everything is alive. We were blessed with a capacity for relational, deep knowing so that we can engage with that aliveness.

Doesn't it make sense that there's a realm of wisdom beyond what our minds can grasp?

Doesn't it make sense that we must have a way of knowing that allows us to connect with and learn from it?

Doesn't it make sense that to experience a creative breakthrough, we must step into Something more expansive than ourselves?

Right now, a global pandemic is still raging, global warming is advancing at an alarming rate, and the gap between the rich and poor is at its highest level in decades. To name just a few issues.

Despite all that, there's a vast living field of intelligence that we haven't even begun to access.

In David Whyte's poem "Sweet Darkness," there is a line: "*Anything or anyone that does not bring you more alive, is too small for you.*" Most of us have focused on things that are too small for us. And for far too long.

We humans have spent hundreds of years relying on our rational thinking process, all the while ignoring our other ways of knowing. *What if we* ***didn't*** *discriminate against deep knowing? What might we see? What discoveries would we make?*

Aren't you curious?

So, here's my request to you: I hope you will begin to sense and perceive the spaciousness that's present with you right now, in this very moment. You don't have to go somewhere to get it. It's right here.

It's time that we notice and value our experiences of deep knowing. Our minds are very clever. They're excellent for writing business plans, developing forecasts, analyzing trends, and managing programs. Of course, we need their abilities. But our minds can't create great art, they can't start global movements, and they can't give us breakthroughs.

They can't even push a tiny crocus through the frozen winter soil.

Your life will change when you allow this realm to work through you. Creative power is everything in this world.

When you've got it, *no one* can take it away from you.

You can spend time learning techniques and strategies for managing your projects, schedules, and lives. You can make checklists, set goals, attend motivational seminars, and get action partners. You can study with experts, read self-help books, and repeat positive affirmations.

Or... you can shift into a place where you are free and creative power can organically flow through you. You have a choice.

I choose freedom.

Potent creative energy wants to flood into our lives and transform us.

CONCLUSION

I was a toddler when the first astronauts landed on the moon, ushering in the golden age of space exploration. Although it's wonderful to learn what's in outer space, I've often wondered why we haven't bothered to explore the extraordinarily intelligent field that's right below the surface of our consciousness. We have an entire realm available for us to study right now, a realm that brings profound and transformative shifts, a realm that is the place of our genius. Developing the capacity to tap its power is more than worthy of our attention.

It seems a silly truism to say that creativity underlies everything that happens in life. But when you ponder that idea, it becomes profound. We live in an animate world; something new always wants to germinate.

Isn't that amazing and inspiring when you really think about it?

The other day, I complained to a friend about how we don't see creativity for what it truly is—the pivotal vehicle behind any change. I complained about our shortsighted cultural focus, a shortsightedness that causes us to dismiss the place from which all true innovation comes.

Then I hung up the phone and began to write. And write and write and write. I had been blocked on a particular project for days; I couldn't put a word down. Suddenly, after a random conversation about the intelligent field, a new writing channel opened up.

The deep creative is our *fuel.*

This beautiful black ooze, this fierce creative power, will take advantage of any opening, any opportunity, any crevice that it can find. Potent creative energy wants to flood into our lives and transform us.

Ultimately, it will be undeterred.

Many years ago, at a particularly low point in my life, I had a vision of an old, worn out, shabby, lonely house filled with ragged, dusty, old furniture. I ascended the stairs to an empty attic except for a wooden chair next to a small table. On the little table was a nondescript little black book. I sat on the chair, opened the book, and out poured wave upon wave of intense, glowing, vibrant beauty. Magnificent colors danced in front of me in the most exquisitely striking patterns I had ever seen. The beauty came out with such force it was almost overwhelming.

When we engage deep knowing, it's like opening that little black book.

To think that we might spend our lives inside that dusty house and all the while there is an ordinary black book up in the attic sitting on a table, just waiting for us to open it.

The intelligent field wants to take you somewhere. It wants to open third space.

AWAKENING DEEP KNOWING #12

WHEN YOU'RE IN FEAR OR OVERWHELM

If you're feeling scared or overwhelmed, go ahead and give yourself a scary image—it could be shattered glass, a gnarly monster, or a bunch of rats running all over the place. Make it horrid.

But *there are two worlds here.* The monsters are in one world—let's put them on the left side. And there's a second world on the right. That world is far, far away from the world with the monsters. As you imagine opening this second world, what image pops up? Since the second world is in an entirely different realm, its image will have a completely different feel from the scary image. It might be a vast meadow or a house or a fairy.

Become the second image. What do you feel? Let's say it's a vast meadow. When I become the vast meadow, I feel EXPANSIVENESS. I'm expanding out in all directions. This is beyond what I can know.

Feel into the source vibration of the second image. Your source vibration might not be expansiveness, but whatever it is is likely bringing you comfort and relief. It's a shift of energy.

Please remember: there's a realm that lies beyond your fear.

Your thinking mind might tell you that this second world is just a fantasy and it's not real. Let me assure you, it's real.

It's more real than your fear.

AWAKENING DEEP KNOWING #13

HELPFUL REMINDERS.

KEEP IT SIMPLE

We humans make things complicated because we think complex things are superior. But complexity is a signal that the thinking mind is involved and that's not where we want to dwell.

When you're present in the moment and connected with deep knowing, how many thoughts do you have in your head? I suspect you have none.

If your image is a tree and you notice its height, what does *tall* mean for you? If your image is a fish and you notice it's slippery, what does *slippery* mean for you? How does slippery help you right now in a situation you've been struggling with?

Keep it simple.

BEWARE OF YOUR NORMAL ASSOCIATIONS

If your image is a castle, what a castle represents in fairy tales is not important. If your image is a surfer, it doesn't mean you're supposed to go surfing. Mental interpretations won't take you anywhere. Simply notice one quality about the image that has nothing to do with what the image means to you. Let that simple quality tell you what you need to know.

TRUST THIS PART OF YOU

When workshop participants tell me they didn't get an image, I usually discover that they *did* get an image. But they didn't think it was the "right" image, so they dismissed it.

Sometimes people in my classes get upset when they get a humble or embarrassing image, while others are getting stately mountains, fireballs in the Universe, or magnificent diamonds. So, they embellish the image with added details or make up a compelling story about it. If they get an apple, they'll turn it into an apple tree. The tennis ball is no longer ordinary; now it's made from titanium. The tumbleweed is no longer a simple piece of brush being blown by the wind. It's now a sacred ceremonial object, intricately connected to the earth. And so on.

I know I've harped on this point in this book, so forgive me for saying it one last time: This is not about what your mind thinks or wants.

You can trust this part of you. A simple, random image is what we're looking for. Simple is GOOD. Simple is POWERFUL.

Accept whatever comes. *It's not what you think.*

DON'T WORRY ABOUT GETTING CLEAR IMAGES

Because you're employing your capacity to *feel* when you work with metaphor, it doesn't matter if you're not great at visualization. You can work with a blob; you can work with a wisp; you can work with something fuzzy. On my own journeys into the field, I never see detailed images anymore. I want to know what I'm *feeling and sensing.* Details are superfluous to where I want to go.

For example, maybe all you get is empty space. Empty is a metaphoric image and we can work with it. There might be nothing to see visually, but there are all kinds of things to feel. Tune into how the image feels and how it wants to move:

Does the emptiness feel full of potential and possibility? Or like a black void? If it's a black void, what does *that* feel like? Does it feel serene? Overwhelming? Expansive? Heavy? Light?

When you feel into it, something that at first appears to be nothing will reveal many layers of meaning.

If the image is unclear, vague, or fuzzy, feel into it. Does the vagueness feel light? Heavy? Cold? Hot? Slow?

Let it slowly reveal itself to you. The cartoonist Lynda Barry says, "The trick is to stand not knowing certain things long enough for them to come to you."

YOU CAN'T THINK YOUR WAY INTO THE FIELD

Our rational minds like to be in charge, so your mind might tell you that you can simply "sit with" the image. (You don't need to "go anywhere.") But to connect with the intelligence of the field, we must go beyond our thinking. The way to do this is to *become* the image, which makes no sense to the mind.

Say you're worried about an upcoming trip and an image of a sturdy bookcase comes to you. You'll get a shift when you take a moment to become the bookcase and you access its source vibration. Just *thinking* of the bookcase won't give you the shift. You need to *feel* its sturdiness; let the cells of your body *know* it.

And don't worry, regardless of whether you believe you have the "right" source vibration, *becoming the image* will take you out of rational thought and into deep knowing.

There's another realm that wants to work with you. Let it.

DON'T VIEW ANY IMAGE AS BAD OR WRONG

If the image feels angry, don't be afraid of the anger. You can trust fierce energy. Step into it and feel what it's like to own this fierceness—it's your *power*. If the image is small, step into the smallness. (As I've mentioned, it can be super comforting to be small. Being small takes the pressure off. It's healing, restful, and refreshing.) If the image is ugly, step into the ugliness and find out what that's about. Ugly might feel interesting, unique, loving, or freeing. Take the time to get to know it.

Whatever quality you notice, let its energy be as big as it wants to be. Let it flood through your body and shift every cell.

You ARE this energy.

LET THE ENERGY GUIDE YOU

Last week I needed to return a phone call, but I didn't feel moved. When I tuned in to deep knowing, the source vibrations were LIGHTNESS, SPACIOUSNESS, and FREEDOM. Those energies confirmed to me that it was fine to not return the call, so I followed that guidance. Later that day, a much better opportunity presented itself. If I had made the earlier phone call, I would have missed out.

On the other hand, if I'd gotten STRONG and CLEARLY DEFINED energy, I would have made the phone call. Strong, clear energy brings clarity and motivates me to act.

Whatever energy is coming through, it's your *answer*.

CHECK IN WITH THE ENERGY DURING THE DAY

It only takes a moment to close your eyes and shift into the image and source vibration you are working with. While you're waiting in line at the grocery store, taking a break at work, or sitting in your car at a stoplight, take a moment to become your image. Even if just for a quick moment, you're allowing another intelligence to be present.

Trust me. No matter how long you spend with it, the intelligent field will work its magic.

HOW DO YOU KNOW YOU HAVE IT RIGHT? BECAUSE IT WILL SHIFT YOU

Yesterday I was feeling sad, confused, and all over the place emotionally. I asked a friend to give me a random image that popped into her head. She said, "A green pea surrounded by purple." That's a strange image, but I went with it.

I felt into its form and my energy shifted.

The green pea was tiny yet surrounded by something pretty (the purple). I found it restful and comforting and something in me relaxed. I felt safe, protected, calm, and centered. Incredibly, I was no longer in the sad, confused place. Those feelings had utterly vanished.

If my rational mind had its way, it would have loudly complained, *"What? A green pea? That doesn't make any sense! Surrounded by purple? That's ridiculous!"* Or *"A green pea is so tiny. I need something big so I can feel better."* Or *"This green pea has nothing to do with my sadness. I want another image!"*

Embrace what doesn't make logical sense. Let it shift you.

Deep knowing does not require magic or extra-sensory abilities. All you're doing is giving your thinking brain a rest so another intelligence can take over.

POSTSCRIPT

In order for us to tap ancient deep inner wisdom we must engage it directly in its aliveness.

~ ELIGIOS S. GALLEGOS

When I was grappling with my shamanic initiation experiences, I picked up a book titled *Shaman Training* from C. Lloyd Thompson and read these words: "There is no such thing as shaman training...The real shaman training is a calling from God." It was helpful and clarifying.

I have a client who thinks she's stuck, but she keeps getting the source vibration of FORM in our sessions, so I know she's not stuck. The intelligent field is urging her to put her ideas and the beauty she knows into *form*—into paintings, poetry, writing, or some other piece of creative work that's entirely her own. I told her, "We value things by putting them into form."

So that's what I have done. I've put the visions and insights that I've been carrying from my shamanic initiations into form. I hope I've done them justice.

I also hope you don't dismiss your own experiences of sacred connection and deep knowing.

If something's alive you can have a relationship with it. And trust me, this realm is alive.

FOR RESEARCH GEEKS

My intent in this supplemental section is to briefly align my work with others who have pursued similar questions. I'm offering this rough summary with the hope of inspiring graduate students or others to seek a better understanding of the intelligent field to further expand our ways of learning and knowing. This is by no means a thorough or comprehensive review. I apologize to those I've neglected to mention.

MARTIN FOSS: METAPHOR AND THE CREATIVE PROCESS

In Chapter 8, I mention fortuitously discovering Martin Foss's book *Symbol and Metaphor in Human Experience.* Upon doing a little research, I discovered that at the time it was published in 1949, *Symbol and Metaphor* was highly acclaimed and prompted some scholars to regard Foss as a greater philosopher than Martin Heidegger (see Armour

& Trott's book, *The Faces of Reason: An Essay on Philosophy and Culture in English Canada.*) But a few short years later, Foss and his work were largely forgotten. In 1956, the *American Scholar* listed *Symbol and Metaphor* as one of the most important and neglected books of the twentieth century. Foss's work deserves more recognition.

SYNESTHESIA: AN AESTHETIC LANGUAGE BENEATH THE SURFACE

The writer Patricia Duffy said that when she was a child, she realized that "to make an R all I had to do was first write a P and then draw a line down from its loop. And I was so surprised that I could turn a yellow letter into an orange letter just by adding a line." This is an example of synesthesia, the capacity to see an aesthetic realm that lies under the surface of our cognitive minds.

Synesthesia is a psychological term that occurs when we blend sensory modalities. People who experience synesthesia can see numbers or words as colors or images, and research suggests that synesthesia is prevalent in 1 out of 23 people. Synesthesia might also occur under the influence of psychedelic drugs, after a stroke, or as a consequence of blindness or deafness. And many artists and writers reportedly dwell in the synesthetic realm.

To my mind, the implications of synesthesia are profound. If *some* of us have the capacity to experience words or numbers in sensory ways, it means that this capacity is likely *available* to all of us...because it's already *there*—under the surface of what we habitually see. There *is* an unconscious aesthetic dimension, and most of the time, we aren't aware of it. Might it be possible that our capacities for metaphoric thinking and our capacities for synesthesia are coming from the same place?

An example of a broader capacity for synesthesia can be found in Wolfgang Kohler's 1929 book, *Gestalt Psychology*, which I mentioned in Chapter 5. In one example, Kohler quotes the German poet Morgenstern who said, "All seagulls look as though their name were Emma," meaning that the sound of the word "Emma" is similar to the visual appearance of a seagull. While synesthesia might seem far removed from normal perception, Kohler's examples demonstrate that there is an aesthetic dimension that we all can tap into.

Synesthesia establishes that *we humans share a common aesthetic language that isn't verbal.* There's a realm of beauty, depth, and complexity beyond what our rational minds can see—under the words, numbers and the other phenomenon of everyday life is an underlying aesthetic pattern. We *do* share a language with the world around us.

There's a basic unconscious aesthetic intelligence and we haven't even begun to access its potential.

FIGURE VERSUS GROUND

Gestalt Psychologists coined the terms *figure* and *ground* to distinguish between what a therapist notices with a client, and what they don't notice. The late media critic and philosopher Marshall McLuhan developed these terms further, broadening the definition of ground to include the whole arena of human attention and perception. He claimed that all cultural situations are composed of an area of attention (figure) and a very much larger area of inattention (ground). In his book *The Global Village*, McLuhan writes:

> "Ground provides the structure of or style of awareness, *the way of seeing* or the terms on which a figure is perceived...The left brain with its sequential, linear bias, hides the ground of most situations, making it subliminal." (Italics are mine).

Metaphor operates as *ground* in our lives—it's the unconscious lens through which we perceive the world.

EMBODIED MIND AND EMBODIED COGNITION

There is a growing field of philosophers, psychologists, and cognitive scientists who believe cognition is a biological phenomenon—shaped in some way by the body. Just a few examples include Bateson, 1979; Maturana and Varela, 1987; Varela et al. 1993; and Lakoff and Johnson, 1999. Michael Polanyi coined the term "tacit knowing" in his book, *The Tacit Dimension.* He writes, "I shall reconsider human knowledge by starting from the fact that we can know more than we can tell." Embodied cognition is allied with metaphor. Metaphor is pre-verbal language.

THE AESTHETIC DIMENSION

Scholar and scientist Gregory Bateson, whose work was ahead of its time, called the realm that lies under our consciousness the *aesthetic dimension.* Aesthetics is about beauty in all its many aspects—referring to a holistic experience that includes both our perceptions and a feeling sense. Perhaps the easiest way to understand it is by experiencing its opposite: anaesthetic—something that produces an absence of sensation or has a dead, mechanical or dry quality. An aesthetic experience is an intimate experience that isn't merely in our heads, but something we can feel in our bodies—a direct, sensual encounter with something that gives us *life*.

For Bateson, the aesthetic dimension is a very real realm of the natural world. He wrote that it comprises a "holistic unity" between our mental processes, culture, and biology that is only comprehensible through metaphor. Mary Catherine Bateson says that her father viewed metaphor as the "main characteristic and organizing glue of this world of mental process." For example, when we look at our hands, we probably first see our five fingers—in other words, five "objects." But we could just as easily look at our hands and see four "connections" between the fingers. Metaphor allows us to see the connections between things.

One of my favorite quotes about Bateson's work is in Kopp's *Metaphor Therapy*:

> It is suggested that long before humans spoke or thought in metaphor, and long before metaphor was the source of novelty and change in language and thought, nature spoke its own language of metaphor—the pattern that connects. Indeed, the metaphoric structure of reality in individuals, families, and within and across cultures may be seen as the expression in humankind of the metaphoric structure underlying the biological evolution of all living things.

Albert Einstein spent time dwelling in the "aesthetic dimension," which he described as "a feeling for the order lying behind the appearance." And Alfred North Whitehead also said that the underlying basis of the world is aesthetic. In his view, all experience is comprised of aesthetic events. Finally, quantum physicists have explored this arena, referring to it as "the field"—a unifying space that "gives shape to matter." Rupert Sheldrake coined the term "morphogenic field."

THIRD SPACE IN JUNGIAN AND DEPTH PSYCHOLOGY

I first came across the term third space in Charles Johnston book, *Necessary Wisdom*, but the concept may also be associated with Jungian and depth psychology. Carl Jung believed there was an "intermediate realm between mind and matter, a psychic realm of subtle bodies" (1968, *The Collected Works of C.G. Jung* Vol. 12). He was fascinated by the ancient art of alchemy where opposites (base metals) unite with the hope of creating a "magical third" (gold) that can transcend ordinary consciousness. Jung believed this process provided a model for understanding inner experience.

Jung also defined something he called the 'transcendent function,' which integrates conscious and unconscious experience into a third state. His method of accessing the third state was through what he called "active imagination" or visioning. Other psychologists have referred to this in-between space as "liminal" and the psychologist Donald Winnicott referred to it as "transitional space" in his book *Transitional Objects and Transitional Phenomena*. He writes: "It is in the space between inner and outer world, which is also the space between people—the transitional space—that intimate relationships and creativity occur."

My writings about third space have also been inspired by the ancient Sufi's and their notion of the imaginal realm. The Islamic scholar Henri Corbin coined the word imaginal to distinguish it from "imaginary." To the ancient Sufis, the imaginal was a *real* world; it was not "made up" or fantasy. The imaginal realm was a real place between spirit and matter where we receive visions and are one with Spirit.

THE HEART'S FIELD OF WISDOM

The ancient Greeks and Sufi mystics both considered the heart to be the true organ of perception. The age-old practice of Chinese medicine focuses on the heart as the center of spiritual energy that expresses our soul. In the field of depth psychology, the heart is considered to be the seat of the imagination, as Henry Corbin writes, "... the heart is the organ which produces true knowledge of things, a knowledge inaccessible to the intellect." And I love the way Stephen Buhner describes it in his book, *Ensouling Language*: "To the ancient cultures, the heart was a sophisticated organ capable of both perception and a unique form of analytical thought, a thought that was oriented around images filled with feeling, a synaesthetic perceptual sensing."

Research from HeartMath Institute and elsewhere demonstrates that our hearts have a brain, with the ability to communicate and process information on their own. For example, Director of Research Rollin McCraty and colleagues write: "[there is] a compelling basis for the proposition that the body accesses a field of potential energy—that exists as a domain apart from space-time reality—into which information about 'future' events is spectrally infolded."

I'm fascinated by this research because it describes what I experience in Doorway sessions. My own experiences of this realm have led me to conclude that metaphor is the language of the heart. It seems likely that when we embody the energy of a metaphor, we enter the heart's field of wisdom. The potent creative energy of the heart field can be seen and felt through metaphor.

APPLICATIONS OF METAPHOR

Metaphor, along with the expanded capacities for learning and knowing of our right hemisphere, opens whole new arenas of research for educators, coaches, and psychologists. I believe these expanded capacities are our next evolution as humans.

NOTES

PREFACE

p. xiv Mihaly Csikszentmihalyi, *Flow: The Psychology of Optimal Experience* (New York: Harper & Row, 1990).

p. xiv Mihaly Csikszentmihalyi & Kim Hermanson, Intrinsic Motivation in Museums: What Makes Visitors Want to Learn? In *Museum News*. (American Association of Museums, 1995).

p. xiv Mihaly Csikszentmihalyi & Kim Hermanson, Intrinsic Motivation in Museums: What Makes Visitors Want to Learn? In *The Educational Role of the Museum* (Eileen Hooper-Greenhill, ed., New York: Routledge, 1999).

p. xiv Mihaly Csikszentmihalyi & Kim Hermanson, Intrinsic Motivation in Museums: Why Does One Want to Learn? Chapter 3 in *Public Institutions for Personal Learning* (John Falk & Lynn Dierking, eds. American Alliance of Museums, 1995).

CHAPTER 1

p. 10 Richard R. Kopp, *Metaphor Therapy* (New York: Routledge, 1995).

p. 11 D.T Suzuki, *A Zen Life*. (Movie directed by Michael Goldberg, Marty Gross Film Productions, 2006.)

p. 18 Margaret Silf, *At Sea with God* (London: Darton, Longman and Todd Ltd, 2003).

CHAPTER 3

p. 41 Martin Foss, *Symbol and Metaphor in Human Experience* (Princeton, NJ: Princeton University Press, 1949).

p. 42 You might check out Gregory Bateson, *Mind and Nature: A Necessary Unity* (London: Wildwood House, 1979). Henry Corbin, *Alone with the Alone: Creative Imagination in the Sufism of Ibn Arabi* (Princeton, NJ: Princeton University, 1997). David Abram, *Spell of the Sensuous: Perception and Language in a More-Than-Human World* (New York: Pantheon Books). George Lakoff and Mark Johnson, *Metaphors We Live By* (Chicago: University of Chicago Press, 1981). Betty Edwards, *Drawing on the Right Side of the Brain* (New York: J.P. Tarcher, 1979). Jerome Bruner, *On Knowing: Essays for the Left Hand* (Boston: Harvard University Press, 1979). Leonard Shlain, *The Alphabet Versus the Goddess: The Conflict Between Word and Image* (New York: Viking, 1998). Jill Bolte Taylor, *My Stroke of Insight* (New York: Penguin, 2008). Bob Samples, *The Metaphoric Mind* (Boston: Addison-Wesley, 1976).

p. 45 Trent Jacobs, *The Authentic Dissertation* (New York: Routledge, 2008).

p. 45 *"divided no more":* Parker Palmer, *The Courage to Teach* (San Francisco: Jossey-Bass, 1998).

CHAPTER 4

p. 51 *"we now truly stand in need"*: Arthur Zajonc, *Goethe's Way of Science: A Phenomenology of Nature* (New York: State University of New York Press, 1998).

p. 56 *"more than I can possibly know"*: Peter Vaill, *Spirited Leading and Learning* (San Francisco: Jossey-Bass, 1998).

p. 56 *"innermost secret of God"*: Martin Foss, *Death, Sacrifice and Tragedy*. (Lincoln, NE: University of Nebraska Press, 1996).

p. 57 *"enter new worlds of the possible"*: Eric Booth, *The everyday work of art* (Lincoln, NE: iUniverse, 1999).

p. 61 *"metaphor is the organizing glue"*: Gregory Bateson and Mary Catherine Bateson, *Angels Fear: Toward an Epistemology of the Sacred* (New York: Macmillan, 1987).

CHAPTER 5

p. 78 *artists notice visual information*: Betty Edwards, *Drawing on the Right Side of the Brain* (New York: J.P. Tarcher, 1979).

p. 81 *two simple line drawings*: Wolfgang Kohler, *Gestalt Psychology* (New York: H. Liveright, 1929).

p. 82 *"Our common human language"*: Rollo May, *My Quest for Beauty* (New York: W.W. Norton & Co., 1985).

p. 83 *"beauty will save the world"*: Dostoevsky, *The Idiot* (New York: Macmillan Company, 1913).

CHAPTER 9

p. 171 *"think small"*: Maira Kalman, *And the Pursuit of Happiness* (New York: Penguin Press, 2010).

CONCLUSION

p. 177 David Whyte, "Sweet Darkness" in *The House of Belonging* (Langley, WA: Many Rivers Press, 1997).

EPILOGUE

p. 193 *"there is no such thing as shaman training"*: C. Lloyd Thompson, *Shaman Training* (C. Lloyd Thompson, 2016).

FOR RESEARCH GEEKS

p. 195 Martin Foss, *Symbol and Metaphor in Human Experience* (Princeton, NJ: Princeton University Press, 1949). Leslie Armour & Elizabeth Trott, *The Faces of Reason: An Essay on Philosophy and Culture in English Canada*

(Waterloo, Ontario: Wilfrid Laurier University Press, 1981). *"The Neglected Books Page" The American Scholar, 1956* (Washington, D.C.: Phi Beta Kappa Society).

p. 196 *"to make an R all I had to do was first write a P"*: Patricia Duffy, *Blue Cats and Chartreuse Kittens: How Synesthetes Color Their Worlds* (New York: Henry Holt & Company, 2001).

p. 197 *"All seagulls look as though their name were Emma"*: Christian Morgenstern. Original quotation cannot be found. Cited by Wolfgang Kohler in *Gestalt Psychology* (New York: H. Liveright, 1929).

p. 198 For more on *figure and ground in Gestalt psychology*: check out https://en.wikipedia.org/wiki/Figure-ground_(perception) or Gestalt psychology in *Encyclopedia Britannica.*

p. 198 *"Ground provides the structure of or style of awareness"*: Marshall McLuhan, *The Global Village* (New York: Oxford University Press, 1989).

p. 199 Gregory Bateson, *Mind and Nature: A Necessary Unity* (New York: Hampton Press, 1979). Humberto Maturana and Francisco

Varela, *The Tree of Knowledge: The Biological Roots of Human Understanding* (Boston, MA: Shambhala, 1987). Francisco Varela, Evan Thompson, and Eleanor Rosch, *The Embodied Mind: Cognitive Science and Human Experience.* (Cambridge, MA: MIT Press, 1991). George Lakoff and Mark Johnson, *Metaphors We Live By* (Chicago: University of Chicago Press, 1980).

p. 199 *"tacit knowing"*: Michael Polanyi, *Personal Knowledge* (Chicago: University of Chicago Press, 1960).

p. 200 Richard R Kopp, *Metaphor Therapy* (England: Routledge, 1995).

p. 201 Charles Johnston, *Necessary Wisdom* (Berkeley, CA: ICD Press, 1991).

p. 201 *"intermediate realm between mind and matter"*: Carl Jung, *The Collected Works of C.G. Jung* (Vol. 12, 1968).

p. 202 *"It is in the space between inner and outer world"*: Donald, Winnicott, "Transitional Objects and Transitional Phenomena" (*International Journal of Psychoanalysis*, 34:89-97).

p. 202 Henri Corbin, *Alone With the Alone: Creative imagination in the Sufism of Ibn Arabi* (Princeton, NJ: Princeton University Press, 1998).

p. 203 *"To the ancient cultures"*: Stephen Buhner, *Ensouling Language* (Rochester, VT: Inner Traditions, 2010).

p. 203 *"the body accesses a field of potential energy"*: Rollin McCraty, Mike Atkinson, & Raymond Trevor Bradley, "Electrophysiological evidence of intuition: Part 1. The surprising role of the heart" (*Journal of Alternative Complementary Medicine, 10(1):* 133-143, 2004).

ABOUT THE AUTHOR

Kim Hermanson, Ph.D. is an author, shaman, and adjunct faculty at Pacifica Graduate Institute. She has taught at many graduate schools and international retreat centers, including the Esalen Institute. Her previous books are *Getting Messy: A Guide to Taking Risks and Opening the Imagination* and *Sky's the Limit: The Art of Nancy Dunlop Cawdrey*, which received an Independent Publisher Book Award. In addition to her own publications, Kim has co-authored articles and book chapters with Mihaly Csikszentmihalyi, author of the *New York Times* bestseller *Flow: The Psychology of Optimal Experience.* Kim worked as a corporate computer scientist in the field of artificial intelligence before a series of shamanic initiation experiences changed the course of her life and launched her calling to expand our human ways of learning and knowing. Her Ph.D. is from the University of Chicago. www.kimhermanson.com

Printed in Great Britain
by Amazon